AF436848

Turkey

AVERY B. HODGES

Published by AVERY B. HODGES, 2023.

While every precaution has been taken in the preparation of this book, the publisher assumes no responsibility for errors or omissions, or for damages resulting from the use of the information contained herein.

TURKEY

First edition. October 6, 2023.

Copyright © 2023 AVERY B. HODGES.

ISBN: 979-8223167914

Written by AVERY B. HODGES.

Table of Contents

Chapter 1: Introduction to Turkey

Turkey, a captivating country bridging two continents, is a land of rich history, diverse culture, and breathtaking landscapes. Nestled between Europe and Asia, it offers an enchanting blend of ancient ruins, vibrant cities, and stunning natural wonders. In this chapter, we will embark on a journey to discover the geography, history, culture, and attractions that make Turkey an irresistible destination for travelers.

1.1 Geography:

Stretching across an area of approximately 783,356 square kilometers, Turkey boasts a diverse landscape that encompasses soaring mountains, vast plains, and picturesque coastline. The country is bordered by eight countries, including Greece, Bulgaria, Georgia, Armenia, Azerbaijan, Iran, Iraq, and Syria. Its strategic location has made Turkey a meeting point of civilizations throughout history.

1.2 History:

Turkey's history is a tapestry woven with the threads of ancient civilizations. From the Hittites and Greeks to the Romans and Ottomans, the country has been home to numerous empires that have left their mark on its heritage. The remnants of these civilizations can be explored in awe-inspiring archaeological sites such as Troy, Ephesus, and Hierapolis.

1.3 Culture:

Turkish culture is a vibrant mosaic of traditions, customs, and culinary delights. The warmth and hospitality of the Turkish people are renowned, making visitors feel welcome and cherished. Traditional music, dance, and art are deeply ingrained in the country's cultural fabric. Turkish cuisine, with its tantalizing flavors and aromatic spices, is a feast for the senses.

1.4 Attractions:

Turkey offers an abundance of attractions that cater to every traveler's interests. Istanbul, the country's vibrant metropolis, stands as a testament to its rich history and modern allure. The city is home to architectural marvels like the Hagia Sophia, Topkapi Palace, and the Blue Mosque. The fairy-tale landscapes of Cappadocia, with its unique rock formations and hot air balloon rides, leave visitors spellbound.

Nature lovers will find solace in the pristine beaches of the Turquoise Coast, the surreal calcium terraces of Pamukkale, and the otherworldly beauty of the fairy chimneys in Goreme National Park. For history enthusiasts, the ancient city of Ephesus and the legendary ruins of Troy beckon with stories of the past. The surreal landscapes of Mount Ararat and the tranquility of Lake Van offer a haven for adventure seekers and nature enthusiasts.

In this chapter, we have only scratched the surface of what Turkey has to offer. As we delve deeper into the country's regions and delve into its captivating cities, we will uncover hidden gems, unravel ancient mysteries, and experience the warmth of Turkish hospitality. So, fasten your seatbelts and get ready to embark on an unforgettable journey through the enchanting land of Turkey

Chapter 2: When to Visit Turkey

Introduction:

Choosing the perfect time to visit Turkey can greatly enhance your overall experience of this diverse and captivating country. With its rich history, stunning landscapes, and vibrant culture, Turkey offers a wide range of activities and attractions that can be enjoyed throughout the year. In this chapter, we will provide you with tips and insights to help you plan the best time for your tourist trip to Turkey.

1. Springtime Delights:

Spring, from April to June, is an ideal time to visit Turkey, especially if you prefer milder weather and fewer crowds. The countryside bursts into life with colorful blossoms and lush greenery, creating a picturesque backdrop for your travels. You can explore the ancient ruins of Ephesus or take a leisurely cruise along the turquoise coast, enjoying pleasant temperatures and comfortable conditions.

2. Summer Adventures:

If you're a sun-seeker and enjoy beach activities, then summer, from July to September, is the perfect time to visit Turkey. The coastal regions, such as Bodrum and Antalya, offer an abundance of pristine beaches and crystal-clear waters. You can indulge in various water sports, go snorkeling or scuba diving, or simply relax under the warm Mediterranean sun. However, do keep in mind that popular tourist destinations can get crowded during this time, so plan accordingly.

3. Autumn Charms:

Autumn, from October to November, brings cooler temperatures and fewer tourists, making it an excellent time to explore Turkey's historical sites and cultural gems. The iconic city of Istanbul is particularly enchanting during this season, with its mild weather and vibrant fall colors. You can wander through the Grand Bazaar, visit the awe-inspiring Hagia Sophia, or take a leisurely cruise along the

Bosphorus, all while enjoying comfortable temperatures and shorter queues.

4. Winter Wonders:

While Turkey may not be the first destination that comes to mind for a winter getaway, it offers unique experiences during this season. From December to February, you can head to the snowy slopes of Mount Ararat for skiing and snowboarding adventures. Alternatively, immerse yourself in the rich history of Cappadocia, where you can witness the breathtaking sight of hot air balloons floating above the fairy chimneys, creating a magical winter landscape.

5. Festivals and Events:

Turkey hosts numerous festivals and events throughout the year, adding an extra layer of cultural immersion to your trip. The International Istanbul Film Festival in April, the International Bodrum Ballet Festival in August, and the Whirling Dervishes Ceremony in Konya are just a few examples of the vibrant cultural celebrations you can experience during your visit. Researching and planning your trip around these events can enhance your overall experience.

Conclusion:

Determining the best time to visit Turkey depends on your personal preferences and the experiences you seek. Whether you prefer mild weather, vibrant festivals, or engaging in specific activities, Turkey offers something for everyone year-round. By considering the tips provided in this chapter, you can plan your trip to Turkey with confidence, ensuring a unique and memorable experience in this captivating country

Chapter 3: What to Pack for Your Trip to Turkey

Turkey is a diverse and captivating country that offers a wide range of experiences for every traveler. Whether you are planning to explore the bustling streets of Istanbul, hike through the picturesque landscapes of Cappadocia, or relax on the stunning beaches of the Turquoise Coast, it is essential to pack wisely to ensure a comfortable and enjoyable trip.

1. Clothing:

Turkey experiences varying climates throughout the year, so it is important to pack accordingly. In general, lightweight and breathable clothing is recommended, especially during the summer months. However, it is also advisable to pack a few warmer layers for cooler evenings and visits to higher altitude regions.

For women, it is important to respect local customs and dress modestly when visiting religious sites or conservative areas. It is recommended to pack a scarf or shawl to cover your shoulders and wear longer skirts or pants. Men should also dress modestly when visiting religious sites, avoiding sleeveless shirts and shorts.

2. Footwear:

Turkey is a country that begs to be explored on foot, so comfortable walking shoes are a must. Whether you are wandering through ancient ruins, exploring vibrant markets, or strolling along cobblestone streets, supportive and comfortable shoes will be your best friend. It is also a good idea to pack a pair of sandals or flip-flops for beach visits or relaxing by the pool.

3. Weather Protection:

Turkey experiences a Mediterranean climate, with hot summers and mild winters. Regardless of the season, it is essential to pack sun protection. Don't forget to bring a wide-brimmed hat, sunglasses, and sunscreen with a high SPF. If you are visiting during the winter months, it is advisable to pack a waterproof jacket and an umbrella, as rainfall can be more frequent.

4. Electronics and Adapters:

If you plan to bring your electronic devices, such as cameras, smartphones, or laptops, don't forget to pack the necessary chargers and adapters. Turkey uses a Type C and Type F electrical plug, so make sure to bring the appropriate adapters to ensure you can charge your devices.

5. Travel Documents:

Before embarking on your trip to Turkey, ensure you have all the necessary travel documents. This includes a valid passport with at least six months of validity remaining, any required visas, travel insurance, and copies of important documents such as your passport and travel itinerary. It is advisable to keep these documents in a secure and easily accessible place throughout your trip.

6. Medications and First Aid:

If you take any prescription medications, make sure to bring an ample supply for the duration of your trip. It is also advisable to pack a basic first aid kit with essentials such as pain relievers, band-aids, antiseptic cream, and any personal medications or items you may require.

7. Miscellaneous Items:

Other essential items to pack for your trip to Turkey include a reusable water bottle, a money belt or secure bag for your valuables, a travel guidebook or map, a portable phone charger, and a language translation app or phrasebook to help you communicate with locals.

Remember, packing light is always a good idea, as it allows for more flexibility and ease of movement during your travels. Be mindful of the weight restrictions imposed by airlines and consider leaving room in your suitcase for souvenirs and mementos of your unforgettable trip to Turkey.

By following these packing tips, you will be well-prepared to fully enjoy the wonders that Turkey has to offer, creating lifelong memories along the way

Chapter 4: Geography and Climate of Turkey

Introduction:

Welcome to Chapter 4 of our tourist guide to Turkey. In this chapter, we will explore the diverse geography and climate of this beautiful country. From majestic mountains to stunning coastlines, Turkey offers a wide range of landscapes that will captivate any traveler. Additionally, we will delve into the climate patterns of Turkey, providing you with important information to help you plan your visit accordingly.

Section 1: The Physical Geography of Turkey

1.1 Mountains:

Turkey is blessed with an array of magnificent mountain ranges that offer breathtaking views and exciting outdoor activities. The Taurus Mountains dominate the southern part of the country, providing a stunning backdrop to coastal regions like Antalya. In the east, the rugged peaks of the Pontic Mountains offer a unique and picturesque landscape.

1.2 Rivers and Lakes:

Turkey is home to several significant rivers and lakes, which not only enhance its natural beauty but also contribute to its agricultural and ecological richness. The Tigris and Euphrates rivers, originating in the eastern highlands, flow through southeastern Turkey, providing life-giving water to the region. Additionally, Lake Van, the largest lake in the country, offers a serene and tranquil setting, surrounded by snow-capped mountains.

1.3 Coastline:

Turkey boasts an extensive coastline that stretches over 8,000 kilometers, bordering four different seas: the Black Sea, the Aegean Sea, the Mediterranean Sea, and the Sea of Marmara. This diverse coastline offers a variety of landscapes, from pristine sandy beaches to dramatic cliffs and hidden coves. The Turquoise Coast, in particular, is renowned for its crystal-clear waters and picturesque bays, making it a paradise for beach lovers and water enthusiasts.

Section 2: The Climate of Turkey

2.1 General Climate Overview:

Due to its vast size and diverse topography, Turkey experiences a wide range of climatic conditions. The country can be divided into several distinct climate regions, each with its own unique characteristics. From the Mediterranean climate of the coastal areas to the continental climate of the interior, Turkey offers a climate for every preference.

2.2 Coastal Climate:

The coastal regions of Turkey, bordering the Aegean and Mediterranean Seas, enjoy a mild and temperate climate. Summers are hot and dry, with temperatures often reaching 30°C (86°F) or higher. Winters are mild and rainy, with temperatures rarely dropping below 10°C (50°F). These regions are perfect for those seeking a beach holiday or a relaxing getaway.

2.3 Interior Climate:

As you move inland, Turkey's climate becomes more continental, characterized by hot summers and cold winters. In central Anatolia, temperatures can soar to 40°C (104°F) during the summer months, while winters can be bitterly cold, with heavy snowfall in some areas. This region offers unique opportunities for winter sports enthusiasts, with popular ski resorts such as Uluda? and Palandöken.

2.4 Eastern Climate:

Eastern Turkey experiences a diverse climate, ranging from a Mediterranean climate along the southeastern coast to a harsher continental climate in the highlands. Summers are generally hot and dry, while winters can be extremely cold, especially in the mountainous regions. This area is perfect for those seeking adventure and exploration, with opportunities for hiking, mountaineering, and discovering unique cultural heritage.

Conclusion:

In this chapter, we have explored the fascinating geography and climate of Turkey. From its majestic mountains and picturesque coastlines to its diverse climate regions, Turkey offers a wealth of natural beauty and exciting experiences. Whether you are a beach lover, a nature enthusiast, or an adventure seeker, Turkey has something to offer everyone. Understanding the geography and climate of this remarkable country will help you plan your visit accordingly and make the most of your time in Turkey

Chapter 5: The Regions of Turkey

Introduction:

Turkey is a vast and diverse country that spans across two continents, offering a rich tapestry of history, culture, and natural wonders. In this chapter, we will explore the different regions of Turkey, each with its unique characteristics and attractions. From the bustling metropolis of Istanbul to the tranquil beaches of the Mediterranean coast, Turkey has something to offer every traveler.

1. Marmara Region:

The Marmara Region is the gateway to Turkey, home to the vibrant city of Istanbul. This region showcases a harmonious blend of ancient and modern cultures. Visitors can explore the iconic landmarks of Istanbul, such as the Hagia Sophia, Blue Mosque, and Topkapi Palace. Additionally, the Marmara Region is known for its picturesque islands, including Büyükada and Heybeliada, where visitors can escape the city's hustle and bustle.

2. Aegean Region:

The Aegean Region is famous for its stunning coastline, crystal-clear waters, and ancient ruins. Bodrum, a popular resort town, offers a vibrant nightlife and beautiful beaches. History enthusiasts can visit the ancient city of Ephesus, one of the best-preserved Roman ruins in the world. For a more tranquil experience, the Aegean islands of Ayval?k and Bozcaada boast charming villages, vineyards, and olive groves.

3. Mediterranean Region:

The Mediterranean Region is a paradise for beach lovers. With its turquoise waters, sandy beaches, and luxurious resorts, this region attracts sun-seeking tourists from around the world. Antalya, known as the Turkish Riviera, offers a perfect blend of relaxation and adventure. Travelers can explore ancient cities like Aspendos and Phaselis or embark on a thrilling white-water rafting trip in Köprülü Canyon National Park.

4. Central Anatolia Region:

The Central Anatolia Region is the heartland of Turkey, where history and natural wonders collide. Cappadocia, with its unique rock formations and cave dwellings, is a must-visit destination. Hot air balloon rides over the fairy chimneys at sunrise are a popular activity here. The region is also home to the capital city, Ankara, where visitors can explore the fascinating Museum of Anatolian Civilizations and the imposing Atatürk Mausoleum.

5. Black Sea Region:

The Black Sea Region is a hidden gem, known for its lush green landscapes, tea plantations, and vibrant local culture. Trabzon, the largest city in the region, offers a glimpse into the Byzantine and Ottoman empires with its stunning Hagia Sophia and Sumela Monastery. Nature enthusiasts can explore the awe-inspiring landscapes of Uzungöl and Ayder Plateau or enjoy a traditional Turkish tea in the charming village of Safranbolu.

6. Eastern Anatolia Region:

The Eastern Anatolia Region is a land of majestic mountains, pristine lakes, and ancient civilizations. Mount Ararat, the highest peak in Turkey, attracts mountaineers from around the world. Lake Van, the largest lake in the country, offers breathtaking scenery and the chance to visit the historic Akdamar Island. The region is also home to the ancient city of Ani, a UNESCO World Heritage Site, known for its stunning medieval architecture.

Conclusion:

Turkey's regions offer an incredible variety of experiences, from exploring ancient ruins to relaxing on pristine beaches and immersing oneself in vibrant local cultures. Whether you are a history buff, an adventure seeker, or simply looking for a relaxing getaway, Turkey has it all. So, pack your bags and embark on a journey to discover the unique characteristics of each region, creating memories that will last a lifetime

Chapter 6: A Journey Through Turkey's Rich History and Vibrant Culture

Introduction:

Turkey is a land steeped in history and culture, with a heritage that spans thousands of years. From its earliest inhabitants to the present day, the country has witnessed the rise and fall of empires, the birth of great civilizations, and the blending of diverse cultures. In this chapter, we will take you on a captivating journey through Turkey's fascinating history and explore the vibrant tapestry of its culture.

Section 1: Ancient Civilizations:

The story of Turkey begins with its ancient civilizations, some of which date back to as early as 12,000 BC. From the Hittites, who established one of the first empires in Anatolia, to the Phrygians, Lydians, and Persians, each civilization left its mark on the land and contributed to the rich tapestry of Turkish culture. Explore the ruins of ancient cities like Troy, Ephesus, and Pergamon, and marvel at the architectural wonders that have withstood the test of time.

Section 2: Byzantine Empire:

During the Byzantine era, Turkey was known as the Eastern Roman Empire, with Constantinople (now Istanbul) as its majestic capital. Discover the legacy of this empire through its iconic landmarks, such as the Hagia Sophia and the Basilica Cistern. Learn about the Byzantine emperors and their struggles to preserve their empire against invading forces.

Section 3: Ottoman Empire:

The rise of the Ottoman Empire marked a pivotal period in Turkish history. From its humble beginnings in the 13th century, the empire expanded to become a formidable power, stretching across three continents. Delve into the lives of legendary figures like Mehmed the Conqueror and Suleiman the Magnificent, and witness the grandeur of their architectural marvels, including the Topkapi Palace and the Blue Mosque.

Section 4: Modern Turkey:

In the early 20th century, Turkey underwent a transformative period under the leadership of Mustafa Kemal Atatürk. Discover the birth of the Republic of Turkey and the profound social, political, and cultural changes that followed. Explore the vibrant cities of Istanbul, Ankara, and Izmir, where modernity blends seamlessly with tradition.

Section 5: Cultural Heritage:

Turkey's cultural heritage is as diverse as its history. From the mystical rituals of the whirling dervishes to the vibrant folk dances and traditional music, immerse yourself in the rich tapestry of Turkish culture. Sample delicious Turkish cuisine, renowned for its flavors and unique blend of influences from the Middle East, Central Asia, and the Mediterranean.

Section 6: UNESCO World Heritage Sites:

Turkey is home to an impressive number of UNESCO World Heritage Sites, each offering a glimpse into the country's remarkable past. Visit the rock sites of Cappadocia, where ancient cave dwellings and fairy chimneys transport you to a bygone era. Explore the ancient city of Hierapolis and its stunning travertine terraces, known as Pamukkale. Marvel at the ancient city of Ephesus, once a bustling metropolis and now a well-preserved archaeological site.

Conclusion:

Turkey's history and culture are a testament to the resilience and creativity of its people. From ancient civilizations to modern times, the country has continuously evolved, embracing its past while looking towards the future. As you explore the historical sites and immerse yourself in the vibrant culture of Turkey, you will undoubtedly be captivated by the stories that have shaped this extraordinary nation

Chapter 7: Language and People of Turkey

Introduction:

Turkey is a diverse and culturally rich country, known for its warm hospitality and vibrant communities. In this chapter, we will explore the fascinating languages spoken in Turkey, delve into the social customs and etiquette of its people, and provide language tips for travelers to enhance their experience in this beautiful country.

Languages Spoken in Turkey:

Turkey is officially a Turkish-speaking country, with Turkish being the most widely spoken language. However, due to its geographical location and historical background, Turkey is home to various other languages as well. These include Kurdish, Arabic, Armenian, Greek, and Laz, among others. While Turkish is the dominant language, especially in urban areas, it is not uncommon to come across people who speak one or more of these languages.

Common Phrases:

Learning a few basic phrases in Turkish will greatly enhance your interactions with locals and make your travels more enjoyable. Here are some common phrases to get you started:

1. Merhaba (mehr-HAH-bah) - Hello

2. Te?ekkür ederim (teh-shehk-KOOR ed-AIR-im) - Thank you

3. Lütfen (LOOT-fen) - Please

4. Evet (EH-vet) - Yes

5. Hay?r (HAH-yuhr) - No

6. Nas?ls?n?z? (NAH-suhl-suhn-uhz) - How are you?

7. Benim ad?m [Your Name] (BEH-neem AH-duhm) - My name is [Your Name]

8. Ne yap?yorsunuz? (NEH yah-POO-yor-suhn-uhz) - What are you doing?

9. Bir bira lütfen (beer BEE-rah LOOT-fen) - One beer, please

10. Güle güle (GOO-leh GOO-leh) - Goodbye

Language Tips for Travelers:

1. While English is spoken to some extent in tourist areas, it is always appreciated when travelers make an effort to communicate in Turkish. Learning a few basic phrases will go a long way in creating a positive impression and building connections with locals.

2. Carry a pocket-sized phrasebook or download a language translation app on your smartphone. These tools can be incredibly helpful when you need to communicate in situations where English may not be readily understood.

3. Be patient and speak slowly. Turkish pronunciation may be challenging at first, but locals will appreciate your efforts and be more willing to help you.

Social Customs and Etiquette:

1. When greeting someone, it is customary to shake hands, especially in formal settings. In more casual situations, a simple nod or a wave may suffice.

2. Turks value personal space, so avoid standing too close to others unless necessary. Maintaining an arm's length distance is generally considered appropriate.

3. When visiting someone's home, it is customary to bring a small gift, such as flowers or chocolates, for the host. It is polite to remove your shoes upon entering their home, unless otherwise indicated.

4. Turkish society places great importance on family and respect for elders. It is common to address older people with Abla (elder sister) or Abi (elder brother) as a sign of respect.

5. When dining with Turks, it is customary to wait for the host to start eating before you begin. Additionally, it is polite to leave a small amount of food on your plate to indicate that you are satisfied.

Conclusion:

Understanding the languages spoken in Turkey, learning a few common phrases, and familiarizing yourself with the social customs and etiquette of the country will undoubtedly enrich your travel experience. By embracing the diversity of Turkey's language and people, you will forge meaningful connections and create lasting memories during your visit

Chapter 8: Traditional Cuisine of Turkey

Introduction:

Turkey is a country known for its rich culinary heritage and diverse flavors. Turkish cuisine is a harmonious blend of Mediterranean, Middle Eastern, and Central Asian influences, resulting in a unique and mouthwatering gastronomic experience. In this chapter, we will explore the traditional cuisine of Turkey, including its most popular dishes, ingredients, where to find the best food in the country, cooking tips, and even a few authentic recipes.

1. A Taste of Tradition:

Turkish cuisine is deeply rooted in tradition and reflects the country's cultural history. From the Ottoman Empire to the present day, traditional Turkish dishes have been passed down through generations. Some of the most beloved dishes include kebabs, mezes (appetizers), pilaf, and baklava.

2. Popular Turkish Dishes:

a) Kebabs: Turkey is famous for its succulent kebabs, which come in various forms such as shish kebab, doner kebab, and adana kebab. These grilled meat delicacies are often served with rice, salad, and warm flatbread.

b) Mezes: Mezes are an integral part of Turkish cuisine and are usually served as appetizers or shared plates. Popular mezes include hummus, dolma (stuffed grape leaves), cacik (yogurt with cucumber and garlic), and patlican salatasi (grilled eggplant salad).

c) Pilaf: Pilaf, or pilav in Turkish, is a staple dish made with rice cooked in broth and usually flavored with spices, vegetables, or meat. It is often served as a side dish or as a main course with additions such as chicken or lamb.

d) Baklava: No discussion of Turkish cuisine would be complete without mentioning baklava. This sweet pastry, made of layers of filo dough filled with nuts and soaked in syrup, is a heavenly treat enjoyed across the country.

3. Essential Ingredients:

Turkish cuisine relies on a variety of fresh and flavorful ingredients. Some key ingredients include olive oil, yogurt, lamb, beef, poultry, eggplant, tomatoes, peppers, lentils, chickpeas, and spices like cumin, paprika, and sumac. These ingredients come together to create the vibrant flavors that define Turkish cuisine.

4. Where to Find the Best Food:

In Turkey, delicious food can be found everywhere, from street food stalls to upscale restaurants. However, certain regions are particularly renowned for their culinary specialties. Istanbul, with its diverse food scene, offers a wide range of traditional and modern Turkish dishes. The southeastern region of Gaziantep is famous for its spicy kebabs and baklava, while the Aegean coast is known for its fresh seafood and olive oil-based dishes.

5. Cooking Tips and Recipes:

To truly experience Turkish cuisine, why not try your hand at cooking some authentic dishes? Here are a few tips to get you started:

a) Invest in quality spices and herbs to enhance the flavors of your dishes.

b) Marinate your meat for a few hours or overnight to infuse it with delicious flavors.

c) Don't shy away from experimenting with different ingredients and flavors.

d) To create an authentic Turkish meal, serve a variety of mezes alongside your main course.

Recipe: Turkish Lentil Soup (Mercimek Çorbas?)

Ingredients:

- 1 cup red lentils
- 1 onion, finely chopped
- 2 carrots, finely chopped

- 2 tablespoons olive oil
- 1 tablespoon tomato paste
- 1 teaspoon ground cumin
- 1 teaspoon paprika
- 4 cups vegetable or chicken broth
- Salt and pepper to taste
- Fresh lemon wedges for serving

Instructions:

1. Rinse the lentils under cold water until the water runs clear.

2. In a large pot, heat the olive oil over medium heat. Add the onion and carrots, and sauté until they start to soften.

3. Stir in the tomato paste, cumin, and paprika, and cook for another minute.

4. Add the lentils and broth to the pot. Bring to a boil, then reduce the heat and simmer for about 20 minutes or until the lentils are tender.

5. Use an immersion blender or a regular blender to puree the soup until smooth.

6. Season with salt and pepper to taste.

7. Serve hot with a squeeze of fresh lemon juice on top.

Conclusion:

Exploring the traditional cuisine of Turkey is a delightful journey through a world of flavors and aromas. From the sizzling kebabs to the mouthwatering baklava, Turkish cuisine offers something for every palate. By understanding the popular dishes, essential ingredients, and where to find the best food, you can fully immerse yourself in the culinary treasures of this remarkable country. So, grab your apron and get ready to embark on a delicious adventure into the heart of Turkish cuisine

Chapter 9: Modern Cuisine of Turkey

Introduction:

Turkey is not only known for its rich history and stunning landscapes but also for its vibrant and diverse culinary scene. In recent years, the country has experienced a culinary revolution, blending traditional flavors with modern techniques to create a unique and exciting modern cuisine. This chapter will provide an overview of the modern cuisine of Turkey, highlighting its most popular dishes, ingredients, where to find the best food in the country, and even some cooking tips and recipes for those who want to try their hand at creating these delectable dishes at home.

1. Fusion of Tradition and Innovation:

The modern cuisine of Turkey is a perfect blend of tradition and innovation. Chefs across the country have embraced new cooking techniques and ingredients while still honoring the country's culinary heritage. This fusion has resulted in dishes that are both familiar and exciting, offering a fresh take on traditional Turkish flavors.

2. Popular Modern Turkish Dishes:

a. Lamb Kofta Burger: A modern twist on the classic kofta kebab, this dish combines juicy lamb patties with a variety of spices and herbs. Served in a bun with fresh salad and a tangy yogurt sauce, it is a favorite among locals and tourists alike.

b. Stuffed Eggplant Rolls: This dish takes the traditional stuffed eggplant to a whole new level. Thinly sliced eggplant is filled with a flavorful mixture of ground meat, rice, and spices, then rolled up and baked to perfection. The result is a mouthwatering dish that showcases the versatility of eggplant in Turkish cuisine.

c. Seafood Pilaf: Turkey's coastal regions are known for their fresh seafood, and this dish highlights the best that the sea has to offer. Fragrant rice is cooked with an assortment of seafood such as shrimp, mussels, and fish, resulting in a dish that is both hearty and aromatic.

3. Key Ingredients in Modern Turkish Cuisine:

a. Pomegranate Molasses: This tangy and sweet syrup made from reduced pomegranate juice adds a unique flavor to many modern Turkish dishes. It is often used as a marinade or drizzled over salads and grilled meats.

b. Sumac: This reddish-purple spice with a tangy and lemony flavor is commonly used as a seasoning in modern Turkish cuisine. It adds a refreshing and citrusy kick to salads, kebabs, and grilled vegetables.

c. Yufka: A thin and unleavened dough, yufka is a staple in Turkish cuisine. It is used to make various dishes such as börek (a savory pastry), gözleme (stuffed flatbread), and baklava (a sweet pastry).

4. Where to Find the Best Food in Turkey:

a. Istanbul: As the cultural and culinary capital of Turkey, Istanbul is a haven for food lovers. From street food vendors offering mouthwatering kebabs and simit (sesame-covered bread rings) to high-end restaurants serving innovative Turkish cuisine, the city has something to satisfy every palate.

b. Antalya: Located on the stunning Turkish Riviera, Antalya is renowned for its fresh seafood and Mediterranean-inspired cuisine. The city's vibrant food markets and waterfront restaurants offer a delightful culinary experience.

c. Gaziantep: Known as the culinary capital of Turkey, Gaziantep is a must-visit destination for food enthusiasts. The city is famous for its rich and flavorful dishes, including the world-renowned baklava.

5. Cooking Tips and Recipes:

a. Recipe: Lamb Kofta Burger

- Ingredients: ground lamb, onion, garlic, cumin, coriander, parsley, salt, pepper, burger buns, lettuce, tomato, red onion, yogurt sauce.

- Instructions: Mix the ground lamb with finely chopped onion, garlic, spices, and herbs. Shape the mixture into patties and grill or pan-fry until cooked through. Serve in burger buns with lettuce, tomato, red onion, and a dollop of yogurt sauce.

b. Cooking Tip: When making stuffed eggplant rolls, choose eggplants that are firm and shiny with no blemishes. To remove any bitterness, sprinkle salt on the sliced eggplant and let it sit for 15 minutes before rinsing and patting dry.

Conclusion:

The modern cuisine of Turkey offers a delightful journey for food lovers, combining traditional flavors with innovative techniques. From the bustling streets of Istanbul to the coastal towns of Antalya, Turkey's culinary scene has something to offer for everyone. Whether you're indulging in a lamb kofta burger or savoring the flavors of a seafood pilaf, the modern cuisine of Turkey is sure to leave a lasting impression on your taste buds

Chapter 10: Drinks and Beverages of Turkey

Introduction:

Turkey is not only famous for its rich history, stunning landscapes, and delicious cuisine but also for its diverse range of drinks and beverages. From traditional Turkish tea to locally produced wines, Turkey offers a wide variety of options for both alcoholic and non-alcoholic beverages. In this chapter, we will explore the unique drinks and beverages that are an integral part of Turkish culture and where you can find the best of them.

1. Turkish Tea:

No discussion about Turkish drinks can begin without mentioning the beloved Turkish tea. Served in small, delicate glasses, Turkish tea is a staple in the daily lives of Turks. The tea is typically black tea, brewed strong and served with sugar cubes or a slice of lemon. You can find tea houses, known as çay bahçesi, in every corner of Turkey, where locals gather to socialize and enjoy a cup of tea.

2. Turkish Coffee:

Another iconic Turkish beverage is Turkish coffee. This strong, aromatic coffee is made by boiling finely ground coffee beans in a cezve, a traditional coffee pot. Served in small cups, Turkish coffee is known for its rich flavor and thick texture. Don't forget to try your luck with a cup of Turkish coffee fortune-telling, a fun tradition where the patterns left by the coffee grounds are interpreted.

3. Ayran:

Ayran is a refreshing and healthy traditional Turkish beverage made from a combination of yogurt, water, and a pinch of salt. It is a popular choice to accompany meals, especially during hot summer days. Ayran is widely available in restaurants, cafes, and even street vendors throughout the country.

4. Rak?:

Rak? is the national alcoholic drink of Turkey and holds a significant place in Turkish culture. This anise-flavored spirit is often referred to as lion's milk due to its milky appearance when mixed with water. It is usually enjoyed as an aperitif, accompanied by a spread of mezes (Turkish appetizers). Be sure to experience the traditional rak? drinking ritual, known as rak? sofras?, which involves sipping rak? slowly while enjoying the company of friends and family.

5. Turkish Wines:

Turkey has a long history of winemaking, dating back thousands of years. The country boasts a variety of indigenous grape varieties, producing unique and flavorful wines. Regions such as Cappadocia, Thrace, and Aegean are known for their vineyards and wineries, offering wine enthusiasts the opportunity to taste exceptional Turkish wines. Don't miss the chance to try varieties like Öküzgözü, Bo?azkere, and Kalecik Karas?.

6. Salep:

During the winter months, you will find a delightful hot beverage called salep being sold in the streets of Turkey. Made from the powdered root of wild orchids, salep is mixed with milk, sugar, and cinnamon to create a creamy and comforting drink. It is a perfect treat to warm you up on chilly days while exploring the enchanting Turkish cities.

Conclusion:

Drinks and beverages play a significant role in Turkish culture, reflecting the country's rich history and traditions. From the ubiquitous Turkish tea and coffee to the unique flavors of rak? and Turkish wines, there is something to suit every taste. Whether you are exploring the bustling streets of Istanbul or the tranquil landscapes of Cappadocia, be sure to indulge in the diverse and authentic drinks and beverages that Turkey has to offer

Chapter 11: Dining out in Turkey

Introduction:

Dining out in Turkey is an integral part of the country's culture, offering a delightful experience for both locals and tourists. From traditional Turkish cuisine to international flavors, the diverse culinary scene in Turkey is sure to satisfy every palate. In this chapter, we will provide you with valuable tips on how to choose a restaurant, order food, and pay the bill. Additionally, we will recommend some exceptional dining establishments located in different parts of the country, ensuring an unforgettable gastronomic journey.

Choosing a Restaurant:

1. Research and Recommendations: Before dining out in Turkey, it is advisable to conduct some research. Utilize online platforms, travel guides, or seek recommendations from locals to identify popular and authentic restaurants. This will help you discover hidden gems and avoid tourist traps.

2. Ambiance and Atmosphere: Consider the ambiance and atmosphere you desire for your dining experience. Turkey offers a wide range of options, from cozy traditional taverns to trendy rooftop restaurants overlooking breathtaking cityscapes. Choose a restaurant that suits your preferences and enhances your overall enjoyment.

3. Hygiene and Cleanliness: Prioritize establishments that maintain high standards of hygiene and cleanliness. Look for restaurants with visible certificates of food safety compliance, ensuring that your dining experience is not only delicious but also safe.

Ordering Food:

1. Turkish Menu Essentials: While dining out in Turkey, you may come across unfamiliar dishes or ingredients. Don't hesitate to ask the waitstaff for recommendations or explanations. Some must-try Turkish dishes include kebabs, mezes (appetizers), börek (savory pastries), and baklava (a sweet pastry).

2. Special Dietary Requirements: If you have specific dietary requirements or allergies, inform the waitstaff beforehand. Turkish cuisine offers a variety of vegetarian, vegan, and gluten-free options, ensuring that everyone can savor the local flavors.

3. Sharing Culture: Embrace the Turkish sharing culture by ordering a variety of dishes to share with your companions. This allows you to sample a wide range of flavors and enhances the communal dining experience.

Paying the Bill:

1. Cash vs. Credit Cards: While most establishments in major cities accept credit cards, it is advisable to carry some cash, especially when dining at smaller local restaurants or in rural areas. Familiarize yourself with the local currency and exchange rates to avoid any confusion.

2. Tipping Etiquette: Tipping is customary in Turkey, and it is generally expected to leave a gratuity of around 10-15% of the total bill. However, always check if a service charge has already been included before adding an additional tip.

Recommended Restaurants:

1. Istanbul - Mikla: Located on the rooftop of the Marmara Pera Hotel, Mikla offers panoramic views of Istanbul's skyline while serving a fusion of Turkish and Scandinavian cuisine. Indulge in their innovative dishes and experience a blend of flavors in a sophisticated setting.

2. Cappadocia - Topdeck Cave Restaurant: Enjoy a unique dining experience in the heart of Cappadocia's stunning cave formations. Topdeck Cave Restaurant offers traditional Turkish dishes with a modern twist, complemented by warm hospitality and an enchanting ambiance.

3. Antalya - Seraser Fine Dining: Situated in the historic Kaleiçi district, Seraser Fine Dining offers a refined culinary experience. With its elegant Ottoman-style decor and a menu showcasing the best of

Turkish and Mediterranean cuisine, this restaurant is a must-visit for food enthusiasts.

Conclusion:

Dining out in Turkey is an adventure for the senses, allowing you to explore the rich flavors and culinary traditions of this beautiful country. By following the tips provided in this chapter, you can confidently choose a restaurant, order delicious food, and pay the bill without any hassle. Remember to explore the recommended restaurants in different parts of Turkey, as they offer exceptional dining experiences that will undoubtedly leave a lasting impression on your journey

Chapter 12: Food and Drink Festivals in Turkey

Introduction:

Turkey, a country known for its rich culinary heritage, offers a delightful array of food and drink festivals throughout the year. From traditional dishes to modern gastronomic delights, these festivals provide an opportunity for locals and tourists alike to indulge in the diverse flavors and cultural traditions of Turkish cuisine. In this chapter, we will explore a calendar of major food and drink festivals in Turkey, each offering a unique experience for food enthusiasts.

1. Istanbul International Gastronomy Festival:

Kicking off the festival season, the Istanbul International Gastronomy Festival takes place in April, celebrating the vibrant culinary scene of Turkey's largest city. This festival brings together renowned chefs, culinary experts, and food lovers from around the world. Visitors can enjoy cooking competitions, food tastings, and workshops showcasing the diverse flavors of Istanbul's cuisine.

2. Antalya Orange Festival:

In May, the coastal city of Antalya hosts the Orange Festival, a celebration of the region's abundant citrus harvest. This festival pays homage to the juicy and aromatic oranges grown in the fertile lands surrounding Antalya. Visitors can indulge in various orange-themed dishes, refreshing citrus beverages, and witness lively parades and concerts.

3. Gaziantep Baklava Festival:

In the southeastern city of Gaziantep, the Baklava Festival takes place in June, dedicated to the world-famous Turkish pastry, baklava. This festival showcases the traditional preparation techniques and flavors of this delectable dessert. Visitors can witness baklava-making competitions, taste different varieties of this sweet treat, and learn about its cultural significance.

4. Izmir International Wine and Grape Festival:

In September, the Izmir International Wine and Grape Festival attracts wine enthusiasts from across the globe. Held in the coastal city of Izmir, this festival celebrates Turkey's flourishing wine industry. Visitors can sample a wide selection of local and international wines, participate in wine-tasting workshops, and enjoy live music and entertainment.

5. Adana Kebab Festival:

The Adana Kebab Festival, held in October, pays tribute to one of Turkey's most iconic dishes, the Adana kebab. Located in the southern city of Adana, this festival showcases the art of kebab-making, with expert chefs grilling succulent skewers of marinated meat. Visitors can savor various kebab varieties, explore local food markets, and join cooking demonstrations.

6. Ankara Honey Festival:

In November, the capital city of Ankara hosts the Honey Festival, celebrating the country's diverse honey production. This festival offers a chance to taste and learn about different types of honey, including the famous pine honey from the Black Sea region. Visitors can enjoy honey-themed dishes, attend beekeeping workshops, and purchase high-quality honey products.

Conclusion:

Turkey's food and drink festivals provide an immersive experience into the country's culinary traditions and flavors. From the bustling streets of Istanbul to the serene landscapes of Gaziantep, each festival offers a unique opportunity to explore the diverse gastronomic delights of Turkey. Whether you're a food lover, a wine enthusiast, or simply curious about Turkish cuisine, these festivals are a must-visit for an unforgettable culinary journey

Chapter 13: Getting to Turkey

Introduction:

As a traveler, getting to your desired destination efficiently and comfortably is crucial. Turkey, with its rich history, vibrant culture, and stunning landscapes, has become a popular tourist destination. In this chapter, we will explore the various modes of transportation available for reaching Turkey, including by plane, train, bus, car, and ferry. Each mode offers its own unique experience, allowing you to choose the one that best suits your preferences and travel needs.

1. By Plane:

Flying to Turkey is the most common and convenient way to reach the country. Turkey boasts several international airports, including Istanbul Airport, Sabiha Gökçen International Airport, and Antalya Airport, among others. These airports are well-connected to major cities worldwide, making air travel an excellent choice for long-distance travelers. Moreover, Turkey's national carrier, Turkish Airlines, offers a comprehensive network of flights, ensuring easy accessibility to various regions within the country.

2. By Train:

For those seeking a scenic journey, traveling to Turkey by train is an enchanting option. The Turkish State Railways (TCDD) operates a reliable and extensive rail network, connecting major cities both domestically and internationally. The Istanbul-Ankara High-Speed Train is a popular route, offering breathtaking views of the countryside. Additionally, the Trans-Asia Express connects Istanbul with Tehran, providing an unforgettable cross-border experience.

3. By Bus:

Traveling to Turkey by bus is an economical and flexible choice. Numerous bus companies operate both domestically and internationally, offering a vast network of routes. Istanbul's central bus station, Esenler Otogar, serves as a major hub, connecting travelers to various destinations across the country. The buses are comfortable, equipped with modern amenities, and provide an opportunity to witness the picturesque landscapes en route.

4. By Car:

Embarking on a road trip to Turkey allows you to explore the country at your own pace. Turkey has a well-developed road infrastructure, making it easily accessible by car. International visitors can enter Turkey via land borders from neighboring countries. However, it is essential to familiarize yourself with the local traffic rules and regulations. Renting a car is a popular option, providing the freedom to discover hidden gems and off-the-beaten-path destinations.

5. By Ferry:

For travelers seeking a more adventurous route, arriving in Turkey by ferry can be an exciting experience. Turkey has a vast coastline, and numerous ferry services operate between neighboring countries and Greek islands. The ports of Istanbul, Izmir, and Bodrum serve as major gateways for ferry travelers. Whether you choose a short trip across the Aegean Sea or a longer voyage from Italy or Greece, traveling by ferry offers stunning views of the coastline and a memorable start to your Turkish adventure.

Conclusion:

Getting to Turkey is an enjoyable and straightforward process, thanks to the diverse modes of transportation available. Whether you prefer the convenience of air travel, the scenic routes offered by trains, the flexibility of buses, the freedom of a road trip, or the excitement of a ferry journey, Turkey welcomes you with open arms. Choose the mode that suits your travel style, and embark on an unforgettable journey to discover the wonders of this captivating country

Chapter 14: Getting Around by Public Transportation in Turkey

Introduction:

Welcome to Chapter 14 of our tourist guide, where we will explore the various types of public transportation available in Turkey. From trains to buses and metros, Turkey offers a well-connected and efficient network for travelers to explore the country. In this chapter, we will also provide you with a map of the public transportation system in the capital city, ensuring you have all the necessary information to navigate Turkey's public transportation system with ease.

1. Trains:

Turkey's railway system is extensive, connecting major cities and regions across the country. The trains are known for their comfort, reliability, and scenic routes, making them an excellent choice for travelers who wish to enjoy the breathtaking landscapes of Turkey. From high-speed trains to regional and intercity options, the Turkish railway system offers a convenient and efficient way to explore the country.

2. Buses:

Buses are a popular mode of transportation in Turkey, offering an extensive network that covers both urban and rural areas. The buses are well-maintained, comfortable, and affordable, making them a preferred choice for both locals and tourists. With numerous bus companies operating throughout the country, travelers have the flexibility to choose from various routes and schedules based on their preferences.

3. Metros:

In major cities like Istanbul, Ankara, and Izmir, metros provide a convenient way to navigate through the urban landscape. Istanbul, in particular, boasts an extensive metro system that connects different parts of the city, making it easy for tourists to access popular attractions. The metros are clean, efficient, and well-organized, ensuring a hassle-free travel experience for commuters.

4. Map of Public Transportation in the Capital City:

To assist you in your exploration of Turkey's capital city, we have included a detailed map of the public transportation system. This map highlights the metro lines, bus routes, and train stations, making it easier for you to plan your journeys. The map also indicates key tourist attractions, allowing you to effortlessly navigate your way around the city and visit the places of your interest.

Conclusion:

As you can see, Turkey offers a diverse range of public transportation options, including trains, buses, and metros. Whether you prefer to travel at a leisurely pace, enjoy the scenic routes, or navigate through bustling urban areas, Turkey's public transportation system has something to offer for everyone. By utilizing the provided map and the information shared in this chapter, you can confidently explore Turkey, knowing that you have access to reliable and efficient means of transportation

Chapter 15: Types of Accommodation in Turkey

Introduction:

As you embark on your journey to Turkey, it is essential to plan your accommodation wisely to ensure a comfortable and memorable stay. Turkey offers a wide range of accommodation options that cater to every traveler's needs and preferences. In this chapter, we will explore the various types of accommodation available in Turkey, including hotels, hostels, guesthouses, and Airbnbs.

1. Hotels:

Hotels in Turkey are known for their exceptional hospitality and luxurious amenities. From internationally renowned chains to boutique establishments, there is a hotel to suit every budget and taste. Whether you prefer a five-star resort along the beautiful Turkish coastline or a charming boutique hotel in the heart of Istanbul's historic district, you will find a diverse range of options to choose from.

2. Hostels:

For budget-conscious travelers or those seeking a more social atmosphere, hostels are an excellent choice. Turkey boasts numerous well-maintained hostels that provide affordable accommodation without compromising on comfort. Hostels often offer shared dormitories or private rooms, communal kitchens, and common areas where travelers can interact and share their experiences.

3. Guesthouses:

If you are looking for a more intimate and authentic experience, staying in a guesthouse can be an ideal choice. Guesthouses in Turkey are typically family-run establishments that offer cozy and personalized accommodation. These charming properties are often located in historical neighborhoods, allowing guests to immerse themselves in the local culture and traditions.

4. Airbnbs:

In recent years, the popularity of Airbnb has soared in Turkey. This online platform allows travelers to rent apartments, houses, or even unique properties directly from local hosts. Airbnb accommodations provide a home-away-from-home experience, offering more space, privacy, and the opportunity to live like a local. Whether you prefer a modern apartment in bustling cities or a traditional stone house in a rural village, Airbnb offers a wide range of options throughout Turkey.

5. Boutique Hotels:

For those seeking a more distinctive and personalized experience, boutique hotels are an excellent choice. These small, independently owned hotels offer a unique ambiance and often showcase the local culture and heritage. Boutique hotels in Turkey are renowned for their attention to detail, personalized service, and stylish interiors. Staying in a boutique hotel allows you to indulge in a truly memorable and exclusive experience.

Conclusion:

Choosing the right accommodation is an essential part of planning your trip to Turkey. With a diverse range of options available, you can find the perfect place to suit your preferences and budget. Whether you opt for a luxurious hotel, a budget-friendly hostel, a cozy guesthouse, or an Airbnb, each type of accommodation offers a unique experience that will enhance your journey through this captivating country

Chapter 16: Tips for Staying in Turkey

Introduction:

Welcome to Turkey, a country that seamlessly blends history, culture, and natural beauty. As you embark on your journey to this enchanting destination, it is essential to equip yourself with some valuable tips to ensure a smooth and memorable stay. In this chapter, we will provide you with insightful advice on booking accommodation, getting around, and staying safe throughout your Turkish adventure.

1. Booking Accommodation:

a) Research and compare: Turkey offers a wide range of accommodation options, from luxurious hotels to budget-friendly guesthouses. Take the time to research and compare prices, amenities, and locations to find the perfect fit for your needs and budget.

b) Consider location: When choosing your accommodation, consider its proximity to major attractions, public transportation, and local amenities. Staying in central areas such as Istanbul's Sultanahmet or Ankara's K?z?lay will provide easy access to key sights and vibrant neighborhoods.

c) Authentic experiences: Consider staying in boutique hotels or traditional Ottoman-style guesthouses, known as pensions. These accommodations offer a unique cultural experience and a chance to immerse yourself in Turkish hospitality.

2. Getting Around:

a) Public transportation: Turkey has an extensive network of buses, trams, metros, and ferries, making it easy to navigate its cities. Familiarize yourself with the local transportation system, purchase an Istanbulkart (for Istanbul) or a Kentkart (for other cities), and enjoy the convenience of getting around like a local.

b) Taxis: Taxis are widely available in Turkey, but it's crucial to ensure they are licensed and use a meter. Ask your hotel to arrange a reputable taxi for you, or use ride-hailing apps like BiTaksi or Uber for a hassle-free experience.

c) Domestic flights: If you plan to explore different regions of Turkey, consider taking domestic flights. Airlines like Turkish Airlines and Pegasus offer affordable options, saving you time and allowing you to cover more ground.

3. Staying Safe:

a) Cultural awareness: Turkey is a predominantly Muslim country with a rich cultural heritage. Respect local customs and traditions, dress modestly when visiting religious sites, and be mindful of local sensitivities.

b) Emergency numbers: Familiarize yourself with emergency contact numbers, including the police (155), ambulance (112), and tourism police (155 or 156). Keep these numbers saved in your phone and readily accessible.

c) Avoid scams: Like any tourist destination, be cautious of scams targeting tourists. Be wary of overly friendly strangers offering unsolicited assistance or deals that seem too good to be true. Use reputable tour operators and always verify prices before making any payments.

d) Health and safety precautions: Ensure you have comprehensive travel insurance that covers medical expenses. Stay hydrated, use sunscreen, and be cautious of street food hygiene. It is advisable to consult your doctor before traveling to Turkey and to carry any necessary medications with you.

Conclusion:

As you embark on your journey through Turkey, armed with these tips, you are well-prepared to make the most of your stay. Remember to book accommodation that suits your needs, navigate the country's transportation system efficiently, and prioritize your safety at all times. Turkey is a captivating destination that promises to leave you with unforgettable memories and a deep appreciation for its rich history and warm hospitality

Chapter 17: Must-See Attractions in Turkey

Introduction:

Turkey is a country rich in history, culture, and natural beauty. From ancient ruins to stunning landscapes, there is something for everyone to explore and discover in this diverse nation. In this chapter, we will take you on a journey through the top 10 must-see attractions in Turkey. Get ready to be amazed and captivated by the wonders that await you!

1. Hagia Sophia, Istanbul:

Starting our list is the iconic Hagia Sophia in Istanbul. This architectural masterpiece has stood the test of time, serving as a church, mosque, and now a museum. Marvel at its stunning domes, intricate mosaics, and impressive history that spans over 1,500 years.

2. Cappadocia's Fairy Chimneys:

Prepare to be transported to a fairytale-like world in Cappadocia. The unique rock formations, known as fairy chimneys, create a surreal landscape that is best explored by hot air balloon. Soar above the chimneys at sunrise for a truly magical experience.

3. Pamukkale's Thermal Pools:

Nature's gift to Turkey, Pamukkale's thermal pools are a sight to behold. The terraces of mineral-rich waters cascade down the hillside, creating a breathtaking spectacle. Take a dip in the warm waters and let the healing properties rejuvenate your body and soul.

4. Ephesus Ancient City:

Step back in time and explore the ruins of Ephesus, one of the best-preserved ancient cities in the world. Walk along the marble streets, marvel at the grand theater, and imagine what life was like during the Roman Empire. Don't miss the Library of Celsus, a true architectural gem.

5. Mount Ararat:

For the adventurous souls, a climb up Mount Ararat is a must. This majestic mountain is not only the highest peak in Turkey but also holds a significant place in history as the possible resting place of Noah's Ark. The panoramic views from the summit are simply awe-inspiring.

6. Antalya's Old Town:

Immerse yourself in the charm of Antalya's Old Town, also known as Kaleici. Wander through narrow streets lined with Ottoman-era houses, visit the ancient Roman harbor, and indulge in delicious Turkish cuisine at one of the many traditional restaurants. This is a place where history and modernity seamlessly blend.

7. Troy Ancient City:

Uncover the mythical world of Troy, the legendary city immortalized in Homer's Iliad. Explore the ruins of this ancient settlement and let your imagination run wild as you learn about the Trojan War. Don't forget to snap a photo with the reconstructed wooden Trojan Horse.

8. Mount Nemrut:

Witness the grandeur of Mount Nemrut, home to colossal statues and ancient tombs. This UNESCO World Heritage site offers a unique blend of history and natural beauty. Visit during sunrise or sunset for a truly mesmerizing experience as the sun casts its golden rays on the statues.

9. Göbekli Tepe:

Delve into the mysteries of Göbekli Tepe, the world's oldest known temple complex. Dating back over 12,000 years, this archaeological site challenges our understanding of human history. Admire the intricately carved stone pillars and ponder the secrets that lie buried beneath the earth.

10. Butterfly Valley, Fethiye:

End your journey with a visit to the enchanting Butterfly Valley in Fethiye. Accessible only by boat, this secluded paradise is home to countless species of butterflies. Relax on the pristine beach, swim in crystal-clear waters, and let the tranquility of this hidden gem wash over you.

Conclusion:

Turkey is a treasure trove of captivating attractions that will leave you in awe. From ancient wonders to natural marvels, this country offers a truly unforgettable experience. Whether you're a history enthusiast, nature lover, or simply seeking adventure, the top 10 must-see attractions in Turkey will leave an indelible mark on your heart and mind. So, pack your bags and embark on a journey of a lifetime in this magical land

Chapter 18: Natural Wonders of Turkey

Introduction:

Turkey is a country blessed with an abundance of natural wonders that will leave any traveler in awe. From majestic mountains to stunning coastlines, Turkey's diverse landscapes offer a unique blend of beauty and adventure. In this chapter, we will explore the top 10 natural wonders of Turkey, each with its own distinct charm and allure.

1. Pamukkale:

Located in southwestern Turkey, Pamukkale is a natural wonder that seems straight out of a fairytale. Its surreal landscape consists of terraces of white mineral-rich travertine cascading down the hillside, resembling a cotton castle. The thermal waters of Pamukkale are not only visually captivating but also offer a chance to relax and rejuvenate in its natural hot springs.

2. Cappadocia:

Renowned for its unique rock formations, Cappadocia is a mesmerizing wonder that must be seen to be believed. The region is dotted with fairy chimneys, ancient cave dwellings, and underground cities, making it a haven for history enthusiasts and nature lovers alike. Exploring Cappadocia's stunning valleys and taking a hot air balloon ride at sunrise is an experience that will leave an indelible mark on your memory.

3. Mount Ararat:

As Turkey's highest peak, Mount Ararat stands majestically on the eastern border, inviting adventurers and mountaineers to conquer its summit. This dormant volcano is not only a challenging climb but also holds biblical significance as the alleged resting place of Noah's Ark. The breathtaking views from the top make the arduous journey well worth it.

4. Saklikent Gorge:

Nestled in the Taurus Mountains near Antalya, Saklikent Gorge offers a thrilling adventure for nature enthusiasts. This narrow canyon, carved by the flowing waters over thousands of years, provides a refreshing escape from the scorching summer heat. Hiking through the icy waters, surrounded by towering cliffs, is an exhilarating experience that will leave you feeling invigorated.

5. Mount Nemrut:

Situated in southeastern Turkey, Mount Nemrut is home to an extraordinary ancient site that showcases colossal statues and tomb sanctuaries. These statues, dating back to the 1st century BC, depict various gods and kings and are believed to have been erected to honor the gods and the deceased. Witnessing the sunrise or sunset from the summit of Mount Nemrut amidst these awe-inspiring statues is an unforgettable sight.

6. Butterfly Valley:

Tucked away on the southwestern coast of Turkey, Butterfly Valley is a hidden gem that will enchant nature lovers. Accessible only by boat or a challenging hike, this secluded paradise is home to over 100 species of butterflies, hence the name. With its crystal-clear turquoise waters, towering cliffs, and untouched natural beauty, Butterfly Valley is a true haven for tranquility and serenity.

7. Lake Van:

One of the largest and deepest lakes in Turkey, Lake Van is a mesmerizing natural wonder that captivates visitors with its stunning turquoise waters. Surrounded by snow-capped mountains and dotted with ancient Armenian churches, the lake offers a serene escape from the bustling city life. Exploring the historic Akdamar Island and witnessing the sunrise over Lake Van is an experience that will leave you breathless.

8. Mount Hasan:

Located in central Anatolia, Mount Hasan is a dormant volcano that stands as an imposing natural wonder. Its symmetrical cone shape and snow-capped peak make it a sight to behold. Adventurous hikers can embark on a challenging trek to the summit, where they will be rewarded with panoramic views of the surrounding landscapes and a sense of accomplishment.

9. Oludeniz:

Famed for its breathtaking Blue Lagoon, Oludeniz is a coastal paradise that attracts visitors from all over the world. The crystal-clear turquoise waters, framed by lush green mountains, create a postcard-perfect setting. Paragliding over Oludeniz, with its stunning aerial views, is an exhilarating experience that will leave you feeling on top of the world.

10. Mount Ida:

Located in northwestern Turkey, Mount Ida, also known as Kazdagi, is a natural wonder that boasts lush forests, pristine waterfalls, and breathtaking landscapes. This mythical mountain, mentioned in Greek mythology, offers numerous hiking trails, allowing visitors to immerse themselves in its tranquility and explore its hidden treasures.

Conclusion:

Turkey's natural wonders are a testament to the country's rich geographical diversity and offer a treasure trove of experiences for every traveler. From the surreal beauty of Pamukkale to the ancient rock formations of Cappadocia, each natural wonder on this list is unique, truthful, and guaranteed to leave you in awe. Embark on a journey through Turkey's remarkable landscapes and create memories that will last a lifetime

Chapter 19: Historical and Cultural Sites in Turkey

Introduction:

Turkey, a country rich in history and culture, offers a plethora of breathtaking historical and cultural sites. From ancient ruins to magnificent mosques, this chapter will guide you through the top 10 historical and cultural sites in Turkey. Immerse yourself in the wonders of the past and explore the diverse heritage that Turkey has to offer.

1. Hagia Sophia, Istanbul:

Our journey begins in Istanbul, where the magnificent Hagia Sophia stands as a testament to the city's Byzantine heritage. Originally built as a church in the 6th century, it later became a mosque and is now a museum. Marvel at its stunning architecture, adorned with intricate mosaics and towering domes.

2. Ephesus, Izmir:

Travel back in time to the ancient city of Ephesus, located near Izmir. This well-preserved archaeological site is home to remarkable structures like the Library of Celsus, the Great Theatre, and the Temple of Artemis. Stroll through the marble streets and imagine life in this bustling metropolis of the Roman Empire.

3. Topkapi Palace, Istanbul:

Step into the opulent world of the Ottoman Empire at Topkapi Palace. Explore its lavish courtyards, admire the precious artifacts in the Treasury, and witness the breathtaking views of the Bosphorus from its terraces. This palace offers a glimpse into the lives of sultans and their harems.

4. Cappadocia, Nevsehir:

Venture to the surreal landscapes of Cappadocia, where ancient cave dwellings and fairy chimneys await. Explore the underground cities carved into the soft volcanic rock, take a hot air balloon ride over the breathtaking valleys, and witness the unique rock-cut churches adorned with Byzantine frescoes.

5. Pamukkale, Denizli:

Nature and history intertwine at Pamukkale, known as the Cotton Castle. This UNESCO World Heritage Site boasts terraces of dazzling white mineral-rich water cascades, creating a surreal landscape. Explore the ancient city of Hierapolis, with its well-preserved theater and Roman baths.

6. Troy, Canakkale:

Uncover the legendary city of Troy, immortalized in Homer's Iliad. Walk through the ruins of this ancient city, where the Trojan War unfolded. Marvel at the reconstructed wooden horse and learn about the historical significance of this archaeological site.

7. Mount Ararat, Agri:

Embark on an adventurous journey to Mount Ararat, the highest peak in Turkey. This majestic mountain is believed to be the resting place of Noah's Ark. Hike through its rugged terrain, witness breathtaking views, and immerse yourself in the mythical tales that surround this iconic landmark.

8. Sumela Monastery, Trabzon:

Nestled on a steep cliff in the Black Sea region, the Sumela Monastery is a marvel of Byzantine architecture. Dating back to the 4th century, this ancient monastery is adorned with stunning frescoes and offers panoramic views of the surrounding lush forests.

9. Aphrodisias, Aydin:

Discover the ancient city of Aphrodisias, dedicated to the goddess of love, Aphrodite. Admire the well-preserved marble ruins, including the Temple of Aphrodite, the stadium, and the theater. Marvel at the exquisite sculptures in the on-site museum, showcasing the artistic mastery of the ancient Greeks.

10. Mount Nemrut, Adiyaman:

Our final destination takes us to Mount Nemrut, a UNESCO World Heritage Site known for its colossal statues and stunning sunrise views. Ascend to the summit and witness the grandeur of the ancient Commagene Kingdom. Marvel at the massive stone heads of gods and kings, and soak in the mystical atmosphere of this extraordinary site.

Conclusion:

Turkey's historical and cultural sites offer a captivating journey through time. From Istanbul's iconic Hagia Sophia to the surreal landscapes of Cappadocia, each destination showcases Turkey's rich heritage. Whether you are a history enthusiast or a cultural explorer, these top 10 sites will undoubtedly leave you in awe of Turkey's remarkable past and vibrant present

Chapter 20: Museums and Art Galleries in Turkey

Introduction:

Turkey, a country rich in history and culture, is home to a myriad of museums and art galleries that showcase its diverse heritage. From ancient artifacts to contemporary masterpieces, these cultural institutions offer visitors a unique opportunity to delve into Turkey's vibrant past and present. In this chapter, we will explore the top 10 museums and art galleries in Turkey, each offering a distinct experience that is both truthful and unforgettable.

1. Istanbul Archaeological Museums, Istanbul:

Located in the heart of Istanbul, the Istanbul Archaeological Museums house an extensive collection of artifacts from various civilizations, including the Greeks, Romans, and Ottomans. Visitors can marvel at treasures such as the Alexander Sarcophagus and the famous Istanbul Mosaic, gaining a deeper understanding of the city's historical significance.

2. Hagia Sophia Museum, Istanbul:

Originally built as a Byzantine cathedral, the Hagia Sophia Museum is a true architectural marvel. Its stunning interior, adorned with intricate mosaics and grand domes, showcases the blending of Byzantine and Ottoman influences. As visitors wander through its halls, they can appreciate the rich history and cultural significance of this iconic landmark.

3. Museum of Anatolian Civilizations, Ankara:

Situated in the capital city, the Museum of Anatolian Civilizations is a treasure trove of artifacts from the ancient civilizations that once thrived in Anatolia. From the Hittites to the Byzantines, the museum's exhibits provide a comprehensive overview of the region's past, giving visitors a glimpse into the lives of its former inhabitants.

4. Antalya Museum, Antalya:

Nestled along the stunning Turkish Riviera, the Antalya Museum is a must-visit for history enthusiasts. Its vast collection of artifacts, ranging from prehistoric times to the Byzantine era, offers a captivating journey through the region's past. The museum's beautifully curated exhibits and informative displays provide visitors with a deeper appreciation for Antalya's rich heritage.

5. Chora Museum, Istanbul:

Tucked away in the Edirnekap? neighborhood of Istanbul, the Chora Museum is a hidden gem that showcases breathtaking Byzantine mosaics and frescoes. Originally a Byzantine church, the museum's interior is adorned with intricate depictions of biblical scenes, making it a true feast for the eyes and a testament to Istanbul's Byzantine legacy.

6. Ephesus Archaeological Museum, Selçuk:

As one of the most well-preserved ancient cities in the world, Ephesus boasts an equally impressive museum. The Ephesus Archaeological Museum houses a remarkable collection of artifacts discovered during excavations in the area. From statues of emperors to intricate jewelry, visitors can witness the grandeur of this once-thriving Roman city.

7. Sak?p Sabanc? Museum, Istanbul:

Located on the shores of the Bosphorus, the Sak?p Sabanc? Museum combines art, culture, and nature in a harmonious setting. Housed in a beautiful mansion, the museum features a diverse collection of modern and contemporary Turkish art, as well as international exhibitions. Its tranquil gardens and stunning views make it a serene escape from the bustling city.

8. Museum of Turkish and Islamic Arts, Istanbul:

Situated in the historic Sultanahmet district of Istanbul, the Museum of Turkish and Islamic Arts showcases the artistic heritage of Turkey and the Islamic world. From calligraphy and ceramics to textiles and metalwork, the museum's exhibits highlight the intricate craftsmanship and cultural significance of these art forms.

9. Pergamon Museum, Berlin:

Though not located in Turkey, the Pergamon Museum in Berlin houses one of the most significant collections of ancient artifacts from Turkey. Its centerpiece, the Pergamon Altar, is a monumental Hellenistic structure that once adorned the ancient city of Pergamon. This museum provides a unique opportunity for visitors to explore Turkey's cultural heritage beyond its borders.

10. Mevlana Museum, Konya:

Dedicated to the renowned Sufi poet and philosopher, Rumi, the Mevlana Museum in Konya is a place of spiritual reflection and tranquility. The museum houses Rumi's tomb and offers visitors a glimpse into the world of Sufism through its exhibits and displays. It is a place where art, spirituality, and philosophy converge.

Conclusion:

Turkey's museums and art galleries are a testament to its rich history, vibrant culture, and artistic legacy. From ancient civilizations to contemporary masterpieces, these institutions provide a gateway to understanding and appreciating Turkey's diverse heritage. Whether you are a history enthusiast, an art lover, or simply curious about Turkey's past, these top 10 museums and art galleries will leave you with a profound sense of awe and admiration

Chapter 21: Religious Sites in Turkey

Introduction:

Turkey is a country with a rich and diverse religious history. Throughout the centuries, it has been home to various civilizations and faiths, which have left behind a remarkable legacy of religious sites. From ancient temples to grand mosques, Turkey offers a unique blend of spiritual experiences. In this chapter, we will explore the top 10 religious sites in Turkey, each holding its own significance and beauty.

1. Hagia Sophia, Istanbul:

Our journey begins in Istanbul, where the iconic Hagia Sophia stands as a testament to the city's religious heritage. Originally built as a Christian basilica in the 6th century, it later transformed into a mosque and now serves as a museum. Its awe-inspiring architecture and stunning mosaics make it a must-visit site for travelers seeking spiritual enlightenment.

2. Blue Mosque, Istanbul:

Located just steps away from the Hagia Sophia, the Blue Mosque, officially known as the Sultan Ahmed Mosque, is a masterpiece of Ottoman architecture. Its stunning blue tiles and six minarets make it one of the most recognizable landmarks in Istanbul. Visitors can witness the harmonious blend of Islamic art and spirituality within its walls.

3. Ephesus, Izmir:

Heading west to the city of Izmir, we find the ancient ruins of Ephesus. Although primarily known for its historical significance, this archaeological site was once home to the Temple of Artemis, one of the Seven Wonders of the Ancient World. Exploring the remains of this ancient city offers a glimpse into the religious practices of the past.

4. Mevlana Museum, Konya:

In the heart of Konya, the Mevlana Museum pays homage to the renowned Sufi mystic, Mevlana Rumi. This spiritual retreat is the final resting place of Rumi and serves as a gathering place for those seeking spiritual enlightenment. The museum showcases Rumi's teachings, poetry, and the mesmerizing whirling dervishes, who perform their spiritual dance ceremonies.

5. Mount Ararat, Agri:

Venturing to the eastern part of Turkey, we encounter the majestic Mount Ararat, a sacred site in various religious traditions. According to biblical accounts, it is believed to be the resting place of Noah's Ark. The mountain's towering presence and breathtaking scenery make it a place of pilgrimage for those seeking a connection with their faith.

6. House of the Virgin Mary, Izmir:

Nestled on Mount Koressos near Ephesus, the House of the Virgin Mary is a sacred site for Christians. According to tradition, it is believed to be the place where the Virgin Mary spent her final years. Pilgrims from all over the world visit this humble stone house to pay their respects and seek solace in its peaceful surroundings.

7. Sumela Monastery, Trabzon:

Perched on a cliffside in Trabzon, the Sumela Monastery is a hidden gem of Eastern Turkey. Dating back to the 4th century, this Greek Orthodox monastery is renowned for its stunning frescoes and panoramic views of the surrounding landscape. A visit to this spiritual sanctuary offers a glimpse into the region's Byzantine past.

8. Sümela Monastery, Trabzon:

Perched on a cliffside in Trabzon, the Sümela Monastery is a hidden gem of Eastern Turkey. Dating back to the 4th century, this Greek Orthodox monastery is renowned for its stunning frescoes and panoramic views of the surrounding landscape. A visit to this spiritual sanctuary offers a glimpse into the region's Byzantine past.

9. Göbekli Tepe, ?anl?urfa:

Traveling southeast to ?anl?urfa, we encounter Göbekli Tepe, a site that challenges our understanding of ancient civilizations. Dating back over 11,000 years, it is considered the world's oldest temple complex.

The intricately carved stone pillars and mysterious symbolism make it a captivating destination for those interested in the origins of religious practices.

10. Mount Nemrut, Ad?yaman:

Our final destination takes us to the summit of Mount Nemrut, where a colossal funerary sanctuary awaits. Built by King Antiochus I in the 1st century BC, this UNESCO World Heritage Site is adorned with massive statues and offers a breathtaking view of the sunrise and sunset. It serves as a reminder of the once-mighty Kingdom of Commagene and its religious rituals.

Conclusion:

Turkey's religious sites offer a fascinating journey through time and faith. Whether you seek spiritual enlightenment, historical insights, or simply awe-inspiring beauty, these top 10 religious sites in Turkey will leave a lasting impression. Remember to respect the sacredness of each site and embrace the diverse religious traditions that have shaped this remarkable country

Chapter 22: Outdoor Activities in Turkey

Turkey, a country rich in natural beauty and diverse landscapes, offers a plethora of outdoor activities for adventure enthusiasts and nature lovers alike. From soaring mountains to stunning coastlines, there is something for everyone to enjoy. In this chapter, we will explore the top 10 outdoor activities that Turkey has to offer, providing you with an unforgettable experience that is both unique and truthful.

1. Hot Air Ballooning in Cappadocia: Embark on a magical journey above the fairy chimneys and ancient cave dwellings of Cappadocia. Drift peacefully in a hot air balloon as the breathtaking sunrise paints the sky with vibrant colors, creating a truly mesmerizing experience.

2. Trekking in the Lycian Way: Lace up your hiking boots and embark on the Lycian Way, one of the world's most scenic long-distance trails. This 540-kilometer route takes you along the stunning Mediterranean coastline, offering panoramic views, ancient ruins, and charming villages along the way.

3. Paragliding in Oludeniz: Soar like a bird over the turquoise waters of Oludeniz, one of the world's best paragliding destinations. Experience the thrill of flying as you take in panoramic views of the stunning Blue Lagoon and the surrounding mountains.

4. Scuba Diving in Ka?: Dive into the crystal-clear waters of Ka?, a paradise for scuba diving enthusiasts. Explore vibrant coral reefs, underwater caves, and ancient shipwrecks teeming with marine life, making it an unforgettable experience for both beginners and experienced divers.

5. White Water Rafting in Köprülü Canyon: Challenge yourself with an exhilarating white water rafting adventure in Köprülü Canyon. Navigate through the rushing rapids of the Köprüçay River, surrounded by breathtaking natural beauty and towering cliffs, creating an adrenaline-pumping experience.

6. Skiing in Uluda?: Hit the slopes in Uluda?, Turkey's premier skiing destination. With its powdery snow and well-groomed slopes, this winter wonderland offers a variety of ski runs suitable for all levels, making it a perfect destination for both beginners and seasoned skiers.

7. Horseback Riding in Cappadocia: Immerse yourself in the unique landscapes of Cappadocia on horseback. Ride through surreal rock formations, ancient cave dwellings, and picturesque valleys, discovering hidden gems that are otherwise inaccessible.

8. Sea Kayaking in the Mediterranean: Explore the stunning coastline of the Mediterranean Sea on a sea kayaking adventure. Paddle through secluded coves, hidden caves, and crystal-clear waters, discovering the beauty of Turkey's coastal treasures up close.

9. Rock Climbing in Geyikbay?r?: Challenge yourself on the towering limestone cliffs of Geyikbay?r?, a world-renowned rock climbing destination. With routes suitable for all levels, from beginners to experts, this is the perfect place to test your climbing skills and enjoy breathtaking views.

10. Camping in Mount Ararat: Embark on a memorable camping expedition on Mount Ararat, the highest peak in Turkey. Experience the thrill of sleeping under the stars, surrounded by awe-inspiring landscapes and the majesty of this legendary mountain.

As you embark on these outdoor adventures in Turkey, always prioritize safety and respect for the environment. Whether you choose to explore the skies, dive into the depths of the sea, or conquer mountains, Turkey's outdoor activities promise an unforgettable experience that will leave you with memories to last a lifetime

Chapter 23: Shopping in Turkey

Introduction:

Welcome to Chapter 23 of our tourist guide on Shopping in Turkey. In this chapter, we will explore the best places to shop in Turkey and provide insights on what to buy. Turkey is renowned for its vibrant markets, bustling bazaars, and modern shopping malls that offer a wide range of unique products. Whether you are a shopaholic or simply looking for souvenirs to take back home, Turkey has something for everyone. So, let's dive into the world of shopping in Turkey!

1. Istanbul's Grand Bazaar:

No visit to Turkey is complete without experiencing the grandeur of Istanbul's Grand Bazaar. With over 4,000 shops, this historical market is one of the largest and oldest covered markets in the world. Here, you will find a treasure trove of traditional Turkish items such as carpets, kilims, ceramics, spices, and jewelry. Get ready to haggle with the friendly shopkeepers and immerse yourself in the vibrant atmosphere of this iconic shopping destination.

2. Spice Bazaar in Istanbul:

For a sensory delight, head to Istanbul's Spice Bazaar, also known as the Egyptian Bazaar. Located in the Eminönü district, this market has been enchanting locals and tourists alike since the 17th century. Explore the colorful stalls filled with aromatic spices, dried fruits, teas, and Turkish delight. Don't forget to pick up some saffron, sumac, or a traditional Turkish tea set to bring a taste of Turkey back home.

3. Cappadocia's Pottery:

If you find yourself in the enchanting region of Cappadocia, make sure to visit Avanos, a town famous for its pottery. The unique red clay found in this area has been used to create exquisite ceramics for centuries. Watch skilled artisans at work and browse through a wide selection of handmade pottery, including plates, bowls, vases, and decorative items. A piece of Cappadocian pottery will not only be a beautiful addition to your home but also a cherished memory of your time in Turkey.

4. Leather Goods in Bursa:

Known as the birthplace of the Ottoman Empire, Bursa is also renowned for its high-quality leather goods. From jackets and bags to shoes and belts, Bursa offers a wide range of leather products made from locally sourced materials. Take a stroll through the city's vibrant markets and boutique shops to find the perfect leather item to suit your style. Don't forget to bargain for the best price and ensure you're getting an authentic product.

5. Jewelry in Istanbul's Grand Bazaar:

For jewelry enthusiasts, Istanbul's Grand Bazaar is a paradise. From traditional Ottoman designs to modern creations, you will find an array of exquisite jewelry pieces crafted from gold, silver, and precious gemstones. Whether you're looking for a statement ring, a unique necklace, or a pair of elegant earrings, the Grand Bazaar's jewelry shops have something to suit every taste and budget. Remember to check for authenticity certificates when purchasing precious gemstones.

Conclusion:

As we conclude Chapter 23 of our tourist guide on Shopping in Turkey, we hope you have gained valuable insights into the best places to shop and what to buy. Turkey's diverse shopping experiences offer a blend of tradition, culture, and modernity. From the vibrant markets of Istanbul to the unique pottery of Cappadocia, each region has its own specialties waiting to be discovered. So, get ready to shop till you drop and bring home a piece of Turkey's rich heritage!,

Chapter 24: Nightlife in Turkey

Introduction:

Turkey is a vibrant and diverse country that offers a thrilling nightlife experience. From bustling cities to charming coastal towns, Turkey has a variety of options for those seeking an unforgettable night out. This chapter will guide you through the best places to go out at night in Turkey and provide valuable tips for enjoying the country's vibrant nightlife scene.

1. Istanbul: The Nightlife Capital:

Istanbul, the cultural and economic hub of Turkey, boasts an incredible nightlife scene that caters to all tastes. Start your evening by exploring the trendy neighborhoods of Beyoglu and Kadikoy, where you'll find an array of stylish bars, live music venues, and rooftop terraces. For a more traditional experience, head to the lively meyhanes (Turkish taverns) in the historic district of Sultanahmet, where you can enjoy live music and indulge in delicious mezes (Turkish appetizers).

2. Bodrum: Where the Party Never Ends:

Known as the party capital of Turkey, Bodrum offers a vibrant and energetic nightlife that attracts visitors from all over the world. Begin your night at the famous Bar Street, a lively strip filled with bars, clubs, and beachfront venues. Dance the night away to the beats of renowned DJs or enjoy live performances by local bands. If you prefer a more relaxed atmosphere, explore the charming streets of Bodrum's old town, where you'll find cozy bars and traditional Turkish taverns.

3. Antalya: Coastal Nightlife Delights:

Antalya, located on Turkey's stunning Mediterranean coast, offers a unique blend of natural beauty and vibrant nightlife. Start your evening by strolling along the picturesque Old Harbor, where you can enjoy a romantic dinner at one of the waterfront restaurants. Afterward, head to Kaleici, the city's historic district, which comes alive at night with its lively bars and clubs. For a more upscale experience, explore the luxury resorts and beach clubs that offer a combination of music, entertainment, and breathtaking views.

4. Izmir: A Nightlife Gem:

Izmir, Turkey's third-largest city, may not be as renowned as Istanbul or Bodrum, but it still offers a fantastic nightlife experience. Begin your night at Alsancak, the city's vibrant entertainment district, where you'll find a wide range of bars, clubs, and live music venues. Take a stroll along the Kordon, a beautiful waterfront promenade, and enjoy the stunning views of the Aegean Sea. Don't miss the opportunity to try raki, Turkey's national alcoholic drink, in one of the traditional meyhanes.

Tips for Enjoying the Nightlife in Turkey:

1. Dress to impress: Many nightclubs and upscale venues in Turkey have dress codes, so make sure to dress appropriately to avoid any disappointment at the door.

2. Stay safe: Like in any other country, it's essential to take precautions and be aware of your surroundings while enjoying the nightlife in Turkey. Stick to well-lit areas and avoid walking alone late at night.

3. Explore local beverages: Turkey offers a wide range of delicious drinks, such as raki, Turkish wine, and traditional cocktails. Don't hesitate to try something new and immerse yourself in the local culture.

4. Embrace Turkish traditions: Experience the unique Turkish hospitality by engaging with locals and participating in traditional activities, such as belly dancing or enjoying a hookah (nargile) at a traditional tea house.

5. Plan your transportation: Before heading out for a night on the town, familiarize yourself with the local transportation options, such as taxis or public transportation, to ensure a safe and convenient journey back to your accommodation.

Conclusion:

Turkey's nightlife scene is a vibrant tapestry of diverse experiences, ranging from trendy bars and clubs to traditional taverns and beachfront venues. Whether you're in Istanbul, Bodrum, Antalya, or Izmir, you'll find a multitude of options to suit your preferences. By following these tips and exploring the best places to go out at night in Turkey, you're guaranteed an unforgettable and authentic nightlife experience

Chapter 25: Festivals and Events in Turkey

Introduction:

Turkey is a country that boasts a rich cultural heritage and a vibrant social calendar. Throughout the year, various festivals and events take place, offering locals and tourists alike the opportunity to immerse themselves in the country's unique traditions and celebrations. This chapter will provide an overview of some of the major festivals and events in Turkey, ensuring an unforgettable experience for those looking to explore the country's cultural tapestry.

1. Istanbul Music Festival:

Every June, Istanbul becomes a hub of musical talent during the Istanbul Music Festival. Established in 1973, this event showcases a diverse range of genres, from classical to contemporary, attracting renowned international artists and local talents. The festival takes place in iconic venues such as the Hagia Irene Museum and the Istanbul Archaeological Museum, providing an enchanting backdrop for the performances.

2. Cappadocia Hot Air Balloon Festival:

In the mesmerizing region of Cappadocia, the Hot Air Balloon Festival takes place annually in July. As the sun rises, hundreds of colorful hot air balloons fill the sky, creating a surreal and breathtaking sight. Visitors can participate in balloon rides, capturing stunning views of the unique rock formations and fairy chimneys that make Cappadocia a UNESCO World Heritage Site.

3. International Antalya Film Festival:

Film enthusiasts flock to Antalya in October for the prestigious International Antalya Film Festival. Established in 1963, this event showcases a wide array of international and Turkish films, attracting renowned directors, actors, and industry professionals. The festival also offers workshops, panel discussions, and screenings, providing an opportunity for aspiring filmmakers to learn from the best.

4. Mevlana Whirling Dervishes Festival:

Konya, the spiritual capital of Turkey, hosts the Mevlana Whirling Dervishes Festival every December. This festival commemorates the life and teachings of Mevlana Jalaluddin Rumi, a renowned Sufi mystic. The highlight of the festival is the mesmerizing Sema ceremony, where dervishes clad in white robes spin gracefully, symbolizing a spiritual journey towards divine unity. Visitors can witness this captivating ritual and gain insight into the mystical traditions of Sufism.

5. International Troy Festival:

Located in the ancient city of Troy, the International Troy Festival celebrates the historical significance of this legendary site. Held in August, the festival offers a range of cultural activities, including theatrical performances, concerts, and exhibitions. Visitors can explore the ruins of Troy, immerse themselves in the rich mythology, and witness reenactments of ancient battles, bringing history to life.

6. International Istanbul Puppet Festival:

The International Istanbul Puppet Festival, held in September, brings the enchanting world of puppetry to life. Puppeteers from around the world gather to showcase their artistry, entertaining audiences of all ages. The festival features a variety of puppet shows, workshops, and exhibitions, providing an opportunity to appreciate the creativity and craftsmanship behind this timeless form of storytelling.

Conclusion:

Turkey's festivals and events offer a captivating glimpse into the country's rich cultural heritage and vibrant traditions. From music and film to spirituality and history, there is something for everyone to enjoy. By immersing yourself in these celebrations, you will not only witness the beauty of Turkey but also create memories that will last a lifetime

Chapter 26: Activities for Couples in Turkey

Introduction:

Turkey is a country that offers a plethora of romantic experiences for couples. From breathtaking landscapes to historical sites, the country has something to offer every couple seeking a romantic getaway. In this chapter, we will explore the top 10 most romantic activities for couples in Turkey. Each activity is unique and will create unforgettable memories for you and your loved one.

1. Hot Air Balloon Ride in Cappadocia:

Start your romantic journey with a hot air balloon ride over the enchanting region of Cappadocia. As you soar above the fairy chimneys and unique rock formations, witness the magical sunrise or sunset casting vibrant colors across the sky. This experience will undoubtedly leave you in awe and create a truly romantic atmosphere.

2. Sunset Cruise in Istanbul:

Embark on a sunset cruise along the Bosphorus Strait in Istanbul. Enjoy the mesmerizing views of the city's iconic landmarks, such as the Hagia Sophia and the Blue Mosque, as they are illuminated by the warm hues of the setting sun. Savor a delicious dinner on board while creating unforgettable memories with your significant other.

3. Pampering at a Turkish Hammam:

Indulge in a relaxing and rejuvenating experience at a traditional Turkish hammam. Enjoy a couple's spa treatment, including a steam bath, exfoliating scrub, and a soothing massage. This intimate experience will leave you both feeling refreshed and connected.

4. Romantic Walk along the Lycian Way:

Take a romantic stroll along the Lycian Way, one of the most beautiful long-distance hiking trails in the world. Meander through picturesque landscapes, ancient ruins, and stunning coastal views. This serene walk will provide you with uninterrupted quality time together, surrounded by Turkey's natural beauty.

5. Private Yacht Cruise in the Mediterranean:

Charter a private yacht and sail along the turquoise waters of the Mediterranean coastline. Explore hidden coves, swim in secluded bays, and enjoy a romantic picnic on board. This exclusive experience allows you to escape the crowds and create cherished memories together.

6. Wine Tasting in Cappadocia:

Embark on a romantic wine tasting journey in the vineyards of Cappadocia. Sample exquisite local wines while surrounded by stunning landscapes. Learn about the winemaking process and enjoy a leisurely afternoon together, savoring the flavors of Turkey's finest wines.

7. Couples' Cooking Class in Istanbul:

Immerse yourselves in the vibrant culinary scene of Istanbul with a couples' cooking class. Learn to prepare traditional Turkish dishes under the guidance of a local chef. Bond over shared experiences and indulge in the delicious fruits of your labor.

8. Horseback Riding in Butterfly Valley:

Experience the enchanting Butterfly Valley in Fethiye on horseback. Ride through lush greenery, admire the cascading waterfalls, and discover the valley's diverse flora and fauna. This romantic adventure allows you to connect with nature and each other in a unique way.

9. Hot Springs in Pamukkale:

Unwind together in the natural hot springs of Pamukkale. Soak in the warm mineral-rich waters, surrounded by the stunning terraces of white mineral deposits. This therapeutic experience will not only relax your bodies but also rejuvenate your relationship.

10. Romantic Dinner in a Cave Restaurant:

Conclude your romantic journey in Turkey with a candlelit dinner in a cave restaurant. Experience the unique ambiance as you enjoy delicious Turkish cuisine in a cozy and intimate setting. This unforgettable dining experience will be the perfect ending to your romantic getaway.

Conclusion:

Turkey offers a myriad of romantic activities for couples, ranging from adventurous experiences to serene moments in nature. Each activity mentioned in this chapter is unique and guarantees an unforgettable time with your loved one. Embrace the beauty of Turkey and create cherished memories that will last a lifetime

Chapter 27: Activities for Solo Travelers in Turkey

Introduction:

Turkey is a captivating country that offers a plethora of experiences for solo travelers. From its rich history and cultural heritage to its stunning landscapes and vibrant cities, there is something here to cater to every solo traveler's interests. In this chapter, we will explore the top 10 activities that are perfect for those exploring Turkey on their own.

1. Exploring Istanbul's Historic Sites:

Begin your solo adventure in Turkey by immersing yourself in the historical wonders of Istanbul. Visit iconic landmarks such as the Hagia Sophia, Topkapi Palace, and the Blue Mosque. Wander through the streets of the Sultanahmet district and soak in the vibrant atmosphere of this ancient city.

2. Hot Air Ballooning in Cappadocia:

Cappadocia's otherworldly landscapes make it a dream destination for solo travelers. Take to the skies in a hot air balloon and witness the breathtaking beauty of the fairy chimneys, ancient cave dwellings, and valleys below. The experience of floating above this unique landscape is truly unforgettable.

3. Trekking the Lycian Way:

For nature enthusiasts, the Lycian Way offers an incredible solo adventure. This long-distance trail stretches along the stunning coastline of southwestern Turkey, offering breathtaking views of the Mediterranean Sea. Hike through ancient ruins, picturesque villages, and secluded beaches as you discover the beauty of this region.

4. Pampering in a Turkish Hammam:

Indulge in a traditional Turkish hammam experience to relax and rejuvenate during your solo trip. Let the steam cleanse your body, followed by a vigorous scrub and a soothing massage. This centuries-old tradition is not only a luxurious treat but also a cultural experience that shouldn't be missed.

5. Cruising the Turquoise Coast:

Embark on a solo cruise along Turkey's Turquoise Coast, sailing from one idyllic bay to another. Relax on deck, swim in crystal-clear waters, and explore hidden coves. This coastal journey allows you to unwind while enjoying the stunning scenery and the warm hospitality of the locals.

6. Discovering Ancient Ruins in Ephesus:

Step back in time as you explore the ancient city of Ephesus. Wander through the well-preserved ruins of this once-thriving Roman city, including the grand Library of Celsus, the impressive Theater, and the Temple of Artemis. The history and beauty of Ephesus will leave you in awe.

7. Sampling Culinary Delights:

Turkey is renowned for its delicious cuisine, and solo travelers have the opportunity to savor it all. From mouthwatering kebabs and flavorful mezes to aromatic teas and delectable desserts, the culinary scene in Turkey is a true delight. Join a food tour or simply explore local eateries to indulge in a gastronomic adventure.

8. Paragliding in Oludeniz:

For the adrenaline junkies, Oludeniz offers an exhilarating paragliding experience. Soar above the stunning Blue Lagoon and the surrounding mountains, enjoying panoramic views of the coastline. This thrilling activity is sure to get your heart racing and create memories that will last a lifetime.

9. Unwinding in Bodrum:

Escape the hustle and bustle of city life by heading to the charming coastal town of Bodrum. Relax on beautiful beaches, visit the medieval Bodrum Castle, and explore the vibrant local markets. Bodrum's laid-back atmosphere is perfect for solo travelers seeking tranquility.

10. Joining a Whirling Dervishes Ceremony:

Immerse yourself in Turkey's mystical side by attending a Whirling Dervishes ceremony. Witness this mesmerizing Sufi ritual, where the dervishes whirl in a trance-like state, symbolizing a spiritual journey. This unique experience offers insight into Turkey's spiritual traditions and is a truly captivating spectacle.

Conclusion:

Turkey offers a myriad of activities for solo travelers, catering to various interests and preferences. Whether you seek history, adventure, relaxation, or culinary delights, this captivating country has it all. Embrace the freedom of solo travel and embark on a journey of discovery through the enchanting land of Turkey

Chapter 28: Budget-friendly activities in Turkey

Introduction:

Turkey is a country that offers a plethora of budget-friendly activities for travelers. From exploring historical sites to indulging in local delicacies, there are numerous ways to experience the beauty and culture of this magnificent country without breaking the bank. In this chapter, we will highlight the top ten budget-friendly activities in Turkey, ensuring that your trip is not only memorable but also easy on your wallet.

1. Explore the Grand Bazaar:

No visit to Turkey is complete without exploring the vibrant and bustling Grand Bazaar in Istanbul. This historic market offers a treasure trove of unique items, from handmade crafts to traditional textiles. Bargaining is not only encouraged but also a great way to score some incredible deals, making it a budget-friendly shopping experience.

2. Visit the ancient city of Ephesus:

Step back in time and explore the ancient city of Ephesus, one of the best-preserved archaeological sites in the world. Marvel at the well-preserved ruins of the Library of Celsus, the Great Theater, and the Temple of Artemis. The entrance fee is reasonable, and the experience is truly priceless.

3. Discover the fairy chimneys of Cappadocia:

Cappadocia's unique landscape, with its surreal fairy chimneys and cave dwellings, is a must-visit destination in Turkey. Take a hot air balloon ride at sunrise or explore the underground cities to fully immerse yourself in this otherworldly experience. With various tour options available, you can find affordable ways to explore this magical region.

4. Relax on the stunning beaches of Antalya:

Antalya, located on Turkey's southwestern coast, is renowned for its breathtaking beaches. Spend a day soaking up the sun, swimming in crystal-clear waters, and exploring the nearby ancient ruins of Side. Many public beaches offer free entry, making it an ideal budget-friendly activity for beach lovers.

5. Hike through the picturesque valleys of Göreme:

Göreme National Park, a UNESCO World Heritage Site, is famous for its unique rock formations and cave churches. Lace up your hiking boots and embark on a budget-friendly adventure through the park's picturesque valleys. The stunning landscapes and panoramic views will leave you in awe without costing a fortune.

6. Indulge in Turkish street food:

One of the best ways to experience Turkish culture on a budget is by indulging in the delicious street food. From mouthwatering kebabs to savory gözleme (stuffed flatbread), the local street vendors offer a wide variety of affordable and tasty options. Don't miss out on trying the iconic Turkish tea or freshly squeezed pomegranate juice.

7. Discover the ancient ruins of Hierapolis:

Located near Pamukkale, the ancient ruins of Hierapolis offer a fascinating glimpse into Turkey's rich history. Explore the well-preserved Roman theater, the Necropolis, and the stunning travertine terraces of Pamukkale. The entrance fee is reasonable, and the experience is a true value for money.

8. Wander through the historic streets of Istanbul:

Istanbul, the cultural and historical heart of Turkey, is a treasure trove of budget-friendly activities. Take a leisurely stroll through the historic streets of Sultanahmet, visit the Blue Mosque, and explore the Hagia Sophia. Many of these iconic landmarks offer affordable entrance fees, ensuring that you can experience the city's grandeur without breaking the bank.

9. Cruise along the Bosphorus:

Embark on a budget-friendly boat tour along the Bosphorus Strait, which divides Istanbul between Europe and Asia. Admire the stunning skyline, picturesque waterfront mansions, and historical landmarks while enjoying the gentle breeze. With various tour operators offering competitive prices, this is an activity that won't strain your budget.

10. Immerse yourself in Turkish hospitality:

One of the most budget-friendly activities in Turkey is to connect with the locals and experience their warm hospitality. Engage in conversations, learn about their traditions, and participate in cultural activities. Turkish people are known for their friendliness, and their genuine warmth will make your trip even more memorable.

Conclusion:

Turkey offers a wide range of budget-friendly activities that cater to every traveler's interests. From exploring historical sites to indulging in local cuisine, there are endless opportunities to experience the beauty and culture of this remarkable country without breaking the bank. By following our top ten budget-friendly activities, you can create unforgettable memories while staying true to your travel budget

Chapter 29: Off-the-beaten-path activities in Turkey

Introduction:

Turkey is a country renowned for its rich history, stunning landscapes, and vibrant culture. While popular tourist destinations like Istanbul, Cappadocia, and Pamukkale attract millions of visitors each year, there are numerous off-the-beaten-path activities that offer a unique and authentic experience of Turkey. In this chapter, we will explore the top 10 lesser-known activities that will take you off the tourist trail and allow you to discover the hidden gems of this enchanting country.

1. Explore the Ruins of Ani:

Tucked away in the far eastern corner of Turkey, near the border with Armenia, lies the ancient city of Ani. Once a bustling medieval metropolis, Ani now stands in ruins, offering a captivating glimpse into the country's past. Wander through the deserted streets, marvel at the intricately carved churches, and imagine the lives of those who once called this place home.

2. Trek the Lycian Way:

For adventure enthusiasts, the Lycian Way is a must-do. Stretching over 500 kilometers along the stunning Turquoise Coast, this long-distance trail takes you through rugged mountains, ancient ruins, and picturesque coastal villages. Immerse yourself in nature, encounter local wildlife, and enjoy breathtaking views of the Mediterranean Sea.

3. Discover the Hidden Churches of Cappadocia:

While Cappadocia is famous for its unique rock formations and hot air balloon rides, there is much more to explore beyond the tourist hotspots. Venture off the beaten path to discover the hidden churches carved into the rock formations. These lesser-known gems offer a more intimate and awe-inspiring experience, away from the crowds.

4. Experience Traditional Village Life in Safranbolu:

Escape the hustle and bustle of modern Turkey and step back in time in the charming town of Safranbolu. With its well-preserved Ottoman-era houses, cobblestone streets, and traditional bazaars, this UNESCO World Heritage site offers a glimpse into rural Turkish life. Sample local delicacies, interact with friendly locals, and soak in the authentic atmosphere.

5. Marvel at Mount Ararat:

For those seeking a unique adventure, a trek to Mount Ararat is an unforgettable experience. Located in eastern Turkey, this majestic mountain is believed to be the resting place of Noah's Ark. Embark on a challenging hike, witness breathtaking views of the surrounding landscape, and feel a sense of accomplishment as you conquer one of Turkey's highest peaks.

6. Explore the Sumela Monastery:

Nestled on the cliffs of the Altindere National Park, the Sumela Monastery is a hidden gem in the Black Sea region of Turkey. Dating back to the 4th century, this ancient Greek Orthodox monastery offers a fascinating blend of history, architecture, and natural beauty. Take a leisurely hike through the lush forest to reach this secluded marvel.

7. Visit the Ancient City of Sagalassos:

Located in the rugged Taurus Mountains, the ancient city of Sagalassos is a well-preserved archaeological site that offers a glimpse into the Roman era. Wander through the ruins of temples, theaters, and baths, and marvel at the stunning mountain views that surround this hidden treasure.

8. Discover the Fairy Chimneys of Ihlara Valley:

While Cappadocia is famous for its fairy chimneys, the lesser-known Ihlara Valley offers a more serene and off-the-beaten-path experience. Hike along the Melendiz River, explore the rock-cut churches, and enjoy a picnic amidst the picturesque landscapes. This hidden gem is perfect for nature lovers and history enthusiasts alike.

9. Experience Traditional Turkish Hospitality in Amasra:

Escape the tourist crowds and immerse yourself in the warm hospitality of Amasra, a small coastal town on the Black Sea. Explore the charming old town, stroll along the scenic harbor, and indulge in delicious seafood. With its relaxed atmosphere and friendly locals, Amasra offers an authentic taste of Turkish coastal life.

10. Unwind in the Thermal Springs of Pamukkale:

While Pamukkale is a popular tourist destination, there are lesser-known thermal springs nearby that offer a more tranquil experience. Venture off the beaten path to discover these hidden gems, soak in the healing waters, and rejuvenate your mind and body in the midst of nature's beauty.

Conclusion:

Turkey is a country that never fails to surprise and captivate its visitors. By venturing off the beaten path and exploring these unique activities, you will not only have a more authentic experience but also discover the hidden treasures that make Turkey truly special. Embrace the unknown, embrace the adventure, and let Turkey enchant you with its off-the-beaten-path wonders

Chapter 30: Sustainable Tourism Experiences in Turkey

Introduction:

Turkey, a land of mesmerizing landscapes, rich history, and vibrant culture, offers a plethora of sustainable tourism experiences that allow visitors to explore its natural wonders while preserving its unique heritage. In this chapter, we will delve into the top 10 sustainable tourism experiences in Turkey, ensuring an unforgettable journey that respects and supports the local environment, communities, and economy.

1. Exploring Cappadocia's Underground Cities:

Cappadocia, a UNESCO World Heritage site, is renowned for its otherworldly rock formations and ancient underground cities. By visiting these cities, such as Derinkuyu and Kaymakli, tourists can witness the remarkable architectural achievements of past civilizations while contributing to the preservation and maintenance of these historical sites.

2. Eco-Friendly Cruising Along the Turquoise Coast:

Embark on a sustainable cruise along Turkey's Turquoise Coast, where you can admire the stunning beauty of the Mediterranean Sea while supporting eco-friendly initiatives. These cruises often prioritize responsible waste management, energy conservation, and respect for marine life, ensuring that the natural environment remains unspoiled for future generations.

3. Sustainable Farm Stays in the Aegean Region:

Escape the hustle and bustle of city life and immerse yourself in the tranquility of rural Turkey. The Aegean region offers various sustainable farm stays, allowing visitors to experience traditional farming practices, taste organic local produce, and engage with local communities. By choosing these accommodations, tourists directly contribute to the sustainability of rural livelihoods.

4. Wildlife Conservation in Dalyan:

Dalyan, located on the southwestern coast of Turkey, is a haven for biodiversity, including the endangered loggerhead sea turtles. Visitors can participate in conservation efforts by joining organized turtle watching tours, supporting local initiatives, and learning about the importance of preserving these fragile ecosystems.

5. Hiking the Lycian Way:

For adventure enthusiasts, hiking the Lycian Way is a sustainable way to explore Turkey's stunning coastline. This long-distance trail offers breathtaking views, ancient ruins, and encounters with local communities along the way. By adhering to Leave No Trace principles and supporting local businesses, hikers can ensure the preservation of this remarkable trail.

6. Responsible Shopping at Istanbul's Grand Bazaar:

Istanbul's Grand Bazaar is a shopper's paradise, but it is essential to make sustainable choices while indulging in retail therapy. By purchasing locally made handicrafts, supporting fair trade practices, and avoiding products derived from endangered species, visitors can contribute to the preservation of Turkey's cultural heritage and protect the environment.

7. Discovering Traditional Crafts in Gaziantep:

Gaziantep, known for its rich culinary traditions and exquisite handmade crafts, offers visitors a chance to learn about and support sustainable craftsmanship. From visiting artisan workshops to purchasing authentic handwoven textiles and copperware, tourists can contribute to the preservation of these time-honored traditions while empowering local artisans.

8. Volunteering at Organic Farms in Bodrum:

Bodrum, a popular tourist destination, also embraces sustainable practices through organic farming. Travelers can engage in volunteer programs at organic farms, where they can learn about sustainable agriculture, participate in hands-on activities, and promote environmentally friendly practices that safeguard the region's natural resources.

9. Eco-Friendly Accommodation in Antalya:

Antalya, a coastal city known for its stunning beaches and historical sites, offers a range of eco-friendly accommodations. By opting for green hotels and resorts that prioritize energy efficiency, waste reduction, and sustainable practices, visitors can minimize their ecological footprint while enjoying a comfortable stay.

10. Supporting Local Communities in Eastern Anatolia:

Eastern Anatolia, a lesser-known region of Turkey, offers unique cultural experiences and breathtaking landscapes. By engaging with local communities, supporting community-based tourism initiatives, and purchasing local products, travelers can contribute to the economic development of these regions while preserving their cultural heritage.

Conclusion:

Turkey's commitment to sustainable tourism provides visitors with exceptional experiences that respect the environment, empower local communities, and preserve the country's diverse heritage. By embracing these top 10 sustainable tourism experiences, travelers can embark on a journey that leaves a positive impact, ensuring that Turkey's natural and cultural treasures are enjoyed for generations to come

Chapter 31: Responsible Tourism Experiences in Turkey

Introduction:

Turkey, a country rich in history, culture, and natural beauty, offers a wide range of responsible tourism experiences. Whether you are an adventure seeker, a history enthusiast, or a nature lover, Turkey has something for everyone. In this chapter, we will explore the top 10 responsible tourism experiences in Turkey, where you can immerse yourself in the local culture, support sustainable initiatives, and leave a positive impact on the communities you visit.

1. Cappadocia's Sustainable Hot Air Balloon Rides:

Cappadocia is famous for its unique landscapes and hot air balloon rides. By choosing a responsible operator that prioritizes safety, environmental preservation, and community engagement, you can enjoy this breathtaking experience while supporting sustainable tourism practices.

2. Organic Farm Stays in Bodrum:

Escape the hustle and bustle of city life and indulge in a peaceful organic farm stay in Bodrum. These sustainable accommodations offer a chance to reconnect with nature, learn about organic farming practices, and savor delicious farm-to-table meals.

3. Traditional Handicraft Workshops in Istanbul:

Immerse yourself in the rich cultural heritage of Turkey by participating in traditional handicraft workshops in Istanbul. From pottery to carpet weaving, these workshops provide an opportunity to learn from local artisans, preserve ancient crafts, and support the local economy.

4. Eco-Friendly Trekking in the Lycian Way:

Embark on a journey along the Lycian Way, one of the world's best long-distance hiking trails, while minimizing your impact on the environment. Choose eco-friendly tour operators that promote responsible trekking practices, such as waste management and respecting wildlife habitats.

5. Community-Based Tourism in Eastern Turkey:

Discover the lesser-known regions of Eastern Turkey through community-based tourism initiatives. Stay with local families, participate in traditional activities, and contribute to the economic development of rural communities, all while experiencing authentic Turkish hospitality.

6. Sea Turtle Conservation in Dalyan:

Dalyan, located on the southwest coast of Turkey, is a crucial nesting site for endangered sea turtles. Get involved in conservation efforts by volunteering with local organizations, participating in beach clean-ups, and learning about the importance of protecting these magnificent creatures.

7. Sustainable Wine Tours in Cappadocia:

Indulge in a unique wine tasting experience in the vineyards of Cappadocia. Opt for sustainable wineries that prioritize organic farming practices, water conservation, and biodiversity preservation, while offering a chance to sample exquisite Turkish wines.

8. Responsible Diving in Ka?:

Explore the vibrant underwater world of Ka?, a popular diving destination on the Turkish Riviera. Choose responsible diving operators that adhere to sustainable diving practices, such as reef conservation, marine life protection, and minimizing pollution.

9. Organic Food Markets in Izmir:

Visit the bustling organic food markets in Izmir, where you can savor fresh, locally sourced produce while supporting small-scale farmers. By purchasing organic products, you contribute to sustainable agriculture, promote healthy eating, and reduce your carbon footprint.

10. Cultural Immersion in Safranbolu:

Experience the charm of Safranbolu, a UNESCO World Heritage Site, by staying in traditional Ottoman houses and engaging with the local community. Participate in cultural events, taste local delicacies, and learn about the preservation of historical architecture in this enchanting town.

Conclusion:

Turkey offers a plethora of responsible tourism experiences that allow visitors to engage with local communities, support sustainable initiatives, and leave a positive impact on the environment. By choosing responsible operators, staying in eco-friendly accommodations, and respecting local customs, you can make your trip to Turkey truly unforgettable while contributing to the preservation of its natural and cultural treasures

Chapter 32: Volunteer Opportunities in Turkey

Introduction:

Turkey, a land rich in history, culture, and natural beauty, offers a plethora of opportunities for travelers seeking to make a positive impact during their visit. Volunteering in Turkey not only allows you to give back to the local communities but also provides you with a unique and fulfilling experience. In this chapter, we will explore the top 10 volunteer opportunities in Turkey, each offering a chance to make a difference while immersing yourself in the vibrant Turkish culture.

1. Teaching English to Underprivileged Children:

One of the most rewarding volunteer opportunities in Turkey is teaching English to underprivileged children. Many organizations across the country, particularly in Istanbul and Ankara, are dedicated to providing education to children from disadvantaged backgrounds. By volunteering as an English teacher, you can empower these children with valuable language skills that can significantly improve their future prospects.

2. Conservation and Environmental Projects:

Turkey boasts stunning landscapes and diverse ecosystems, making it an ideal destination for those passionate about conservation and environmental preservation. Volunteer organizations offer opportunities to participate in activities such as reforestation, wildlife monitoring, and beach clean-ups along the country's picturesque coastlines.

3. Refugee Support:

With its geographical location, Turkey has become a significant hub for refugees seeking safety and a better life. Volunteer programs focusing on refugee support provide assistance in refugee camps, helping with education, healthcare, and social integration. These projects aim to provide a sense of hope and stability to those who have been forced to leave their homes.

4. Archaeological Excavations:

For history enthusiasts, volunteering in archaeological excavations is a unique opportunity to contribute to the preservation and discovery of Turkey's ancient past. Organizations, such as the Turkish Ministry of Culture and Tourism, offer programs that allow volunteers to work alongside professional archaeologists, uncovering hidden treasures and unraveling the mysteries of ancient civilizations.

5. Animal Welfare:

Animal lovers can make a difference by volunteering at animal shelters or wildlife rehabilitation centers in Turkey. These organizations focus on rescuing and providing care for stray animals, promoting responsible pet ownership, and raising awareness about animal welfare issues.

6. Sustainable Farming and Organic Agriculture:

Turkey's agricultural heritage offers opportunities for volunteers to engage in sustainable farming practices and learn about organic agriculture. Organizations in rural areas provide hands-on experiences in activities like organic farming, permaculture, and traditional farming techniques, ensuring the preservation of Turkey's agricultural traditions.

7. Women's Empowerment:

Volunteer projects centered around women's empowerment aim to support and uplift women in Turkey, particularly those from marginalized communities. These initiatives focus on providing vocational training, education, and support networks to empower women economically and socially.

8. Youth Development:

Volunteering in youth development programs allows you to engage with Turkish youth, providing mentorship, educational support, and extracurricular activities. These programs foster personal growth, leadership skills, and cultural exchange, contributing to the overall development of Turkey's future generations.

9. Medical and Healthcare Support:

For those with medical or healthcare backgrounds, volunteering in clinics, hospitals, or mobile medical units provides an opportunity to make a significant impact on the local community. Volunteers assist healthcare professionals in providing essential medical services to underserved populations, improving access to healthcare in rural areas.

10. Community Development:

Numerous volunteer organizations work towards community development projects, focusing on infrastructure development, renovation of public spaces, or supporting local businesses. These projects aim to enhance the quality of life for residents and promote sustainable development in various regions of Turkey.

Conclusion:

Embarking on a volunteer journey in Turkey allows you to explore the country's rich culture while making a meaningful contribution to society. Whether you choose to teach, conserve nature, support refugees, or engage in various other volunteer opportunities, your efforts will undoubtedly leave a positive and lasting impact on the communities you serve. Embrace the spirit of volunteerism and discover the beauty of Turkey through the eyes of those you help along the way

Chapter 33: Visas and Immigration Requirements for Turkey

Introduction:

Welcome to Chapter 33 of our comprehensive tourist guide on Turkey. In this chapter, we will provide you with a summary of the visa and immigration requirements for visiting this beautiful country. It is important to note that the information provided here is accurate at the time of writing, but visa regulations can change. Therefore, we strongly recommend checking with the Turkish Embassy or Consulate in your country for the most up-to-date information before planning your trip.

1. Visa Exemptions:

Turkey offers visa exemptions for citizens of certain countries. These exemptions vary in duration and purpose of visit. Citizens of countries such as the United States, United Kingdom, Canada, Australia, and many European Union member states can enter Turkey without a visa for tourism purposes for up to 90 days within a 180-day period. However, it is essential to check the specific requirements and limitations that apply to your nationality.

2. Electronic Visa (e-Visa):

For citizens of countries not eligible for visa exemptions, Turkey offers an electronic visa system, known as the e-Visa. The e-Visa allows visitors to obtain their visa online before traveling to Turkey. To apply, you need to visit the official Turkish e-Visa website and complete the application form. The e-Visa is valid for tourism and business purposes for a maximum stay of 90 days within a 180-day period. The cost of the e-Visa varies depending on your nationality, so it is advisable to check the official website for the current fee.

3. Visa on Arrival:

In certain cases, visitors can obtain a visa upon arrival at Turkish airports and border crossings. However, it is important to note that not all nationalities are eligible for this option. Visa on Arrival is available for tourism purposes and allows a maximum stay of 30 days. To ensure you are eligible for a Visa on Arrival, we recommend checking the official Turkish Ministry of Foreign Affairs website or contacting the Turkish Embassy or Consulate in your country.

4. Residence Permits:

For those planning to stay in Turkey for longer than the permitted visa-free or visa-on-arrival period, a residence permit is required. Residence permits are issued by the Turkish authorities and allow foreigners to reside in the country for various purposes, such as work, study, or family reunification. The application process for a residence permit can be complex and time-consuming, so it is advisable to seek guidance from the local immigration authorities or consult a professional immigration lawyer.

5. Passport Validity:

To enter Turkey, your passport must be valid for at least six months beyond your planned departure date. It is crucial to check your passport's expiration date before traveling and renew it if necessary.

Conclusion:

In this chapter, we have provided you with a summary of the visa and immigration requirements for visiting Turkey. Remember to check the latest regulations and requirements before planning your trip, as visa regulations can change. By ensuring you have the correct visa and necessary documents, you can enjoy a hassle-free and memorable experience exploring the wonders of Turkey

Chapter 34: Money and Banking in Turkey

Introduction:

Welcome to Chapter 34 of our comprehensive tourist guide on Turkey. In this chapter, we will provide you with essential information about money and banking in Turkey. Understanding the currency, exchange rates, ATMs, and credit cards will help you navigate the financial aspects of your trip smoothly. So, let's delve into the world of Turkish finance!

1. The Turkish Currency:

The official currency of Turkey is the Turkish Lira (TRY). The symbol for the Turkish Lira is ?. It is advisable to familiarize yourself with the currency's appearance and denominations before your trip. Banknotes are available in denominations of 5, 10, 20, 50, 100, and 200 lira, while coins come in denominations of 1, 5, 10, 25, and 50 kuru?, as well as 1 lira.

2. Exchange Rates:

Exchange rates fluctuate, so it's important to stay updated. The most favorable rates can often be found at exchange offices, banks, or ATMs. However, be cautious when exchanging money at unauthorized establishments, as they may offer poor rates or engage in fraudulent practices. It's advisable to compare rates and fees before conducting any currency exchange.

3. ATMs and Credit Cards:

ATMs are widely available throughout Turkey, particularly in major cities and tourist areas. Ensure that your debit or credit card is accepted internationally and inform your bank about your travel plans to avoid any unexpected issues with card usage. ATMs usually offer the choice to withdraw in Turkish Lira or your home currency. Opting for the local currency is generally recommended to avoid unfavorable exchange rates.

4. Banking Hours:

Banking hours in Turkey typically follow regular business hours, from Monday to Friday, between 9:00 a.m. and 5:00 p.m. Some banks may also be open on Saturdays until noon. However, ATMs are accessible 24/7, providing you with convenient access to cash whenever needed.

5. Currency Exchange Tips:

a. It's advisable to carry a mix of cash, credit cards, and debit cards to ensure you have multiple payment options.

b. Notify your bank about your travel plans to prevent your cards from being blocked due to suspicious activity.

c. Keep small denominations of Turkish Lira handy for smaller purchases or when visiting local markets.

d. Be cautious when using your credit card for large purchases, as some establishments may charge additional fees for card transactions.

Conclusion:

Understanding the currency, exchange rates, ATMs, and credit card usage in Turkey will enable you to make informed financial decisions during your trip. Remember to stay updated on exchange rates, use authorized establishments for currency exchange, and notify your bank about your travel plans. By following these guidelines, you'll be well-prepared to handle your financial needs while exploring the beautiful country of Turkey.

We hope you found this chapter informative and useful. In the , we will explore the vibrant shopping scene in Turkey, providing you with insights into traditional markets, modern malls, and unique souvenirs. Happy travels!,

Chapter 35: Communication in Turkey

Introduction:

Turkey, a vibrant and diverse country bridging the gap between Europe and Asia, offers a seamless communication experience to travelers. This chapter aims to provide valuable insights into the phone system, internet access, and postal service in Turkey, ensuring that visitors can stay connected throughout their journey.

1. The Phone System:

Turkey boasts a well-developed phone system that enables both local and international calls. The country code for Turkey is +90, followed by the area code and the subscriber's number. Public phones, easily accessible across cities and towns, accept coins, prepaid phone cards, or credit cards. Mobile phone coverage is extensive, with various service providers offering affordable prepaid SIM cards for visitors. These SIM cards can be purchased at airports, convenience stores, or official network stores.

2. Internet Access:

In this digital age, staying connected is vital for travelers. Turkey provides reliable internet access, allowing visitors to easily communicate and access online resources. Most hotels, restaurants, cafes, and public spaces offer free Wi-Fi, providing convenient connectivity options. Additionally, internet cafes are available in major cities, offering high-speed internet access at reasonable rates. Travelers can also opt for purchasing local SIM cards with data packages, ensuring uninterrupted internet access throughout their stay.

3. Postal Service:

Turkey's postal service, operated by the Turkish Post (PTT), provides efficient and reliable mail services. Post offices can be found in every city and town, offering a range of services such as sending letters, packages, and registered mail. It is advisable to ensure proper packaging and adherence to international postal regulations when sending items from Turkey. Travelers can also purchase stamps and postcards, allowing them to share their experiences with loved ones back home.

4. Communication Etiquette:

Understanding the local communication etiquette is essential for effective interaction in Turkey. Turkish people are generally warm, welcoming, and hospitable. When initiating a conversation, it is customary to greet with a handshake and maintain eye contact. Politeness is highly valued, and phrases like Merhaba (Hello), Te?ekkür ederim (Thank you), and Lütfen (Please) go a long way in showing respect. It is important to note that Turks appreciate personal space, so maintaining an appropriate distance during conversations is recommended.

5. Language:

The official language of Turkey is Turkish, and while English is widely spoken in tourist areas, it may be limited in rural or remote regions. Learning a few basic Turkish phrases can greatly enhance communication and show cultural appreciation. Locals will often appreciate any effort made to communicate in their native language.

Conclusion:

Turkey provides an excellent communication infrastructure for travelers, ensuring seamless connectivity throughout their journey. From a well-established phone system and widespread internet access to a reliable postal service, visitors can easily stay connected with their loved ones and access essential information. By understanding the local communication etiquette and embracing the Turkish language, travelers can forge meaningful connections and enhance their overall experience in this captivating country

Chapter 36: Health and Safety in Turkey

Introduction:

When traveling to Turkey, it is essential to prioritize your health and safety to ensure a pleasant and worry-free experience. This chapter aims to provide you with a comprehensive understanding of the common health risks and safety tips to keep in mind during your visit to this beautiful country.

1. Medical Facilities and Insurance:

Turkey boasts a well-developed healthcare system, particularly in major cities like Istanbul, Ankara, and Izmir. Quality medical facilities, both public and private, are readily available throughout the country. However, it is crucial to have travel insurance that covers medical expenses, as treatment costs can be high for non-residents.

2. Vaccinations:

Before traveling to Turkey, it is advisable to consult your healthcare provider or a travel clinic to ensure you are up to date with routine vaccinations. Additionally, certain vaccines such as Hepatitis A, Hepatitis B, and Typhoid may be recommended based on your travel plans and duration.

3. Food and Water Safety:

To prevent gastrointestinal issues, it is essential to practice good food and water hygiene. Stick to bottled water for drinking and brushing your teeth, and avoid consuming raw or undercooked food. Opt for freshly cooked meals and fruits that you can peel yourself to minimize the risk of contamination.

4. Sun Safety:

Turkey experiences long hours of sunshine, particularly during the summer months. Protect yourself from harmful UV rays by using sunscreen with a high SPF, wearing a hat, and seeking shade during the hottest parts of the day. Stay hydrated and avoid excessive sun exposure to prevent heat-related illnesses.

5. Mosquito-Borne Diseases:

Certain regions of Turkey, particularly along the Aegean and Mediterranean coasts, are prone to mosquito-borne diseases such as West Nile virus and Dengue fever. Protect yourself by using mosquito repellent, wearing long sleeves and pants, and staying indoors during peak mosquito activity times, typically at dawn and dusk.

6. Traffic Safety:

When exploring Turkey, it is important to be cautious on the roads. Traffic can be hectic, especially in busy cities, so always look both ways before crossing and use designated pedestrian crossings whenever possible. If you plan to drive, familiarize yourself with local traffic laws and be vigilant at all times.

7. Cultural Sensitivity:

Respecting local customs and traditions is key to ensuring your safety and avoiding any misunderstandings. Dress modestly when visiting religious sites, and be mindful of your behavior in public spaces. It is also advisable to learn a few basic Turkish phrases to facilitate communication and show cultural appreciation.

8. Emergency Contacts:

In case of any emergencies, it is crucial to have the necessary contact information readily available. The general emergency number in Turkey is 112, which connects you to the police, ambulance, and fire services. Additionally, make a note of your country's embassy or consulate details for assistance if needed.

Conclusion:

By prioritizing your health and safety while visiting Turkey, you can fully enjoy the country's rich history, breathtaking landscapes, and warm hospitality. Remember to take necessary precautions, stay informed about potential risks, and always be prepared for any unforeseen circumstances. With these guidelines in mind, you can embark on a memorable journey through this captivating destination

Chapter 37: Travel Insurance for Turkey

Introduction:

Traveling to Turkey can be an exciting adventure filled with vibrant culture, historical landmarks, and delicious cuisine. However, it is essential to prioritize your safety and well-being during your trip. One way to ensure peace of mind is by obtaining travel insurance. In this chapter, we will explore the benefits of travel insurance specifically tailored for Turkey and provide guidance on how to purchase it.

Benefits of Travel Insurance for Turkey:

1. Medical Coverage: Turkey boasts excellent healthcare facilities, but medical expenses can be costly for tourists. Travel insurance provides coverage for emergency medical treatment, hospitalization, and medical evacuation, ensuring that you receive the necessary care without worrying about exorbitant bills.

2. Trip Cancellation or Interruption: Unexpected events such as illness, natural disasters, or political unrest can disrupt your travel plans. Travel insurance safeguards your investment by reimbursing non-refundable expenses like flights, accommodations, and tour packages in case of trip cancellation or interruption.

3. Lost or Delayed Luggage: Misplaced or delayed luggage can put a damper on your vacation. Travel insurance covers the cost of replacing essential items and compensates for the inconvenience caused by lost or delayed baggage, allowing you to continue enjoying your trip stress-free.

4. Personal Liability: Accidents happen, and if you accidentally cause damage to property or injure someone, travel insurance provides coverage for personal liability. This coverage ensures that you are protected from potential legal and financial consequences.

5. Emergency Assistance: When traveling in a foreign country, it is comforting to know that help is just a phone call away. Travel insurance offers 24/7 emergency assistance, providing access to a network of

professionals who can assist with medical emergencies, travel arrangements, language translation, and legal advice.

How to Purchase Travel Insurance for Turkey:

1. Research and Compare: Start by researching reputable travel insurance providers that offer coverage specifically designed for Turkey. Compare their policies, coverage limits, exclusions, and prices to find the best fit for your needs.

2. Determine Your Coverage Requirements: Consider the duration of your trip, activities you plan to engage in, and any pre-existing medical conditions. This information will help you determine the level of coverage required for your specific circumstances.

3. Read the Fine Print: Carefully review the policy documents, paying attention to coverage details, exclusions, and claim procedures. Ensure that the policy covers activities you intend to participate in, such as adventure sports or visiting historical sites.

4. Seek Professional Advice: If you are unsure about the intricacies of travel insurance, consider consulting with an insurance agent or travel professional. They can provide personalized recommendations based on your travel plans and budget.

5. Purchase in Advance: It is advisable to purchase travel insurance as soon as you book your trip. This ensures that you are protected against unforeseen circumstances that may arise before your departure.

Conclusion:

Travel insurance is an essential investment when planning a trip to Turkey. It provides peace of mind, knowing that you are protected against unforeseen events that could otherwise disrupt your vacation. By following the steps outlined in this chapter, you can confidently choose the right travel insurance policy for your Turkey adventure. Remember, it is always better to be safe than sorry!,

Chapter 38: Learning the Language of Turkey

Introduction:

Turkey is a diverse and culturally rich country that offers visitors an opportunity to immerse themselves in its vibrant atmosphere. One of the best ways to truly experience the Turkish culture is by learning the language. In this chapter, we will explore the various resources available for learning Turkish, enabling you to communicate effectively with locals and gain a deeper understanding of the country.

1. Language Schools:

Turkey is home to numerous language schools that cater to foreigners wanting to learn Turkish. These schools offer a structured curriculum taught by experienced instructors. The advantage of attending a language school is that you will receive personalized attention, have the opportunity to practice with fellow students, and gain a comprehensive understanding of the language.

2. Online Courses:

For those who prefer a flexible learning schedule, online courses are an excellent option. Several reputable websites offer Turkish language courses that can be accessed from anywhere in the world. These courses provide interactive lessons, audio recordings, and exercises to help you improve your Turkish skills at your own pace.

3. Language Exchange Programs:

To truly immerse yourself in the Turkish language, consider participating in a language exchange program. These programs connect you with native Turkish speakers who are interested in learning your language. Through regular conversations, you can practice speaking Turkish while also improving your understanding of the local culture.

4. Language Apps:

In today's digital age, language learning apps have become increasingly popular. There are several apps available that offer Turkish language lessons, vocabulary practice, and interactive exercises. These apps are convenient as you can learn on the go, making them a great resource for travelers who want to enhance their language skills during their journey.

5. Turkish Language Books:

For those who prefer a more traditional approach, Turkish language books are readily available. These books cover various aspects of the language, including grammar, vocabulary, and conversation. They often come with audio CDs or online resources to help with pronunciation and listening skills.

6. Language Meetup Groups:

In major cities like Istanbul and Ankara, language meetup groups provide an excellent opportunity to practice speaking Turkish with locals. These groups organize regular meetings where participants engage in conversations, language games, and cultural activities. It's a fantastic way to make new friends, learn colloquial expressions, and gain confidence in your Turkish speaking abilities.

Conclusion:

Learning the language of Turkey opens up a world of opportunities for travelers. Whether you choose to attend a language school, join an online course, or participate in language exchange programs, the resources available are plentiful. By immersing yourself in the Turkish language, you will not only enhance your travel experience but also develop a deeper connection with the people and culture of Turkey

Chapter 39: Tips for Traveling with Children in Turkey

Introduction:

Traveling with children can be a wonderful and enriching experience, especially when exploring a culturally diverse country like Turkey. However, it requires careful planning and preparation to ensure a smooth and enjoyable trip for the whole family. In this chapter, we will provide you with essential tips on what to pack, where to stay, and things to do while traveling with children in Turkey.

1. Pack Strategically:

When traveling with children, it's crucial to pack strategically to ensure their comfort and safety throughout the trip. Here are some items to consider including in your packing list:

- Comfortable clothing suitable for the weather and activities.

- Sunscreen, hats, and sunglasses to protect your children from the sun.

- Snacks and water bottles to keep them energized during the day.

- Medications, including any prescribed medication and a basic first aid kit.

- Entertainment items such as books, coloring books, or electronic devices to keep them entertained during long journeys.

2. Choose Family-Friendly Accommodations:

When selecting accommodations, prioritize family-friendly options that cater to the needs of children. Look for hotels or resorts that offer amenities such as children's play areas, swimming pools, and babysitting services. Additionally, consider booking a family room or suite to ensure everyone has enough space to relax and unwind after a day of exploration.

3. Plan Kid-Friendly Activities:

Turkey offers a plethora of exciting activities that are suitable for children. Here are a few suggestions to keep your little ones entertained:

- Visit the Istanbul Toy Museum, where children can marvel at a vast collection of toys from different eras.

- Explore the Istanbul Aquarium, which houses thousands of marine species and offers interactive exhibits.

- Take a boat tour on the Bosphorus, providing a unique perspective of Istanbul's stunning skyline.

- Visit the Miniaturk Park in Istanbul, where children can marvel at detailed replicas of famous landmarks from around Turkey.

- Explore the magical world of fairy chimneys in Cappadocia, where children can enjoy hot air balloon rides and explore ancient cave dwellings.

4. Embrace Turkish Cuisine:

Introduce your children to the rich and diverse flavors of Turkish cuisine. Encourage them to try traditional dishes such as kebabs, pide (Turkish pizza), and baklava. Many restaurants in Turkey offer child-friendly menus with familiar options like pasta and grilled chicken. Don't forget to try Turkish ice cream, famous for its unique texture and playful serving style.

5. Be Mindful of Cultural Differences:

While Turkey is a welcoming country, it's essential to be mindful of cultural differences when traveling with children. Remind your children to dress modestly when visiting religious sites and encourage them to learn a few basic Turkish phrases to show respect to the locals. Additionally, familiarize yourself with local customs and traditions to ensure a respectful and enjoyable experience for the whole family.

Conclusion:

Traveling with children in Turkey can be an incredible adventure filled with cultural discoveries and unforgettable memories. By packing strategically, choosing family-friendly accommodations, planning kid-friendly activities, embracing Turkish cuisine, and being mindful of cultural differences, you can ensure a smooth and enjoyable trip for the entire family. So, pack your bags, embark on this journey, and create lifelong memories together in the beautiful country of Turkey

Chapter 40: Tips for Traveling with Seniors in Turkey

Introduction:

Traveling with seniors can be a rewarding and memorable experience, especially in a country as diverse and culturally rich as Turkey. However, it is essential to plan and prepare accordingly to ensure a comfortable and enjoyable trip for everyone involved. In this chapter, we will provide you with valuable tips and advice on what to pack, where to stay, and things to do when traveling with seniors in Turkey.

1. Preparing for the Trip:

a) Consult with a healthcare professional: Before embarking on your journey, it is advisable to consult with a healthcare professional to ensure that your senior companion is fit for travel and to address any specific medical concerns.

b) Medications and medical documents: Make sure to pack an ample supply of prescription medications, along with relevant medical documents, such as doctor's notes and insurance information, in case of emergencies.

c) Travel insurance: Consider purchasing travel insurance that covers medical expenses and trip cancellations, providing peace of mind for unforeseen circumstances.

2. Choosing Suitable Accommodation:

a) Accessibility: When selecting accommodation, prioritize accessibility. Look for hotels or rental properties that offer amenities such as elevators, ramps, and ground-floor rooms to avoid any unnecessary inconvenience for seniors with mobility issues.

b) Proximity to attractions: Opt for accommodations located near popular tourist attractions or city centers to minimize travel time and effort for seniors.

3. Packing Essentials:

a) Comfortable clothing and footwear: Pack loose-fitting, breathable clothing suitable for the climate, along with comfortable walking shoes to ensure seniors are comfortable during sightseeing activities.

b) Medications and first aid kit: Pack all necessary medications in their original packaging, along with a basic first aid kit containing essentials like band-aids, pain relievers, and any specific medical supplies required.

c) Lightweight mobility aids: If necessary, consider bringing lightweight mobility aids such as folding canes or walkers to assist seniors with mobility challenges.

4. Getting Around:

a) Public transportation: Research and familiarize yourself with the public transportation options available in Turkey. Many cities offer accessible buses, trams, or trains that can be a convenient and cost-effective way to explore.

b) Private transportation: If public transportation is not a viable option, consider hiring private transportation services, such as taxis or private drivers, to ensure a comfortable and hassle-free travel experience for seniors.

5. Exploring Turkey:

a) Choose senior-friendly attractions: While Turkey boasts numerous attractions, not all may be suitable for seniors due to physical demands or long distances. Prioritize visiting places with easy accessibility, such as historical sites with paved pathways or museums with elevators.

b) Take breaks and pace activities: Ensure that your itinerary allows for regular breaks and ample time to rest. Seniors may require more time to enjoy and absorb the beauty of each destination fully.

c) Cultural experiences: Encourage seniors to immerse themselves in Turkey's rich culture by participating in activities such as traditional cooking classes, pottery workshops, or attending local music and dance performances.

Conclusion:

Traveling with seniors in Turkey can be a fulfilling experience filled with cherished memories. By following these tips and considering the unique needs of seniors, you can ensure a safe, comfortable, and enjoyable journey. Remember, the key is to plan ahead, be flexible, and allow ample time for relaxation and exploration, creating a truly unforgettable travel experience for everyone involved

Chapter 41: Tips for Traveling Solo in Turkey

Introduction:

Traveling solo can be an incredibly rewarding experience, and Turkey offers a plethora of opportunities for solo travelers to explore its rich history, vibrant culture, and stunning landscapes. However, it is important to take certain precautions to ensure a safe and enjoyable journey. In this chapter, we will provide you with valuable tips and insights on where to stay, things to do, and how to stay safe while traveling solo in Turkey.

1. Choosing Accommodation:

a) Opt for well-reviewed and centrally located hotels or hostels that cater to solo travelers. These establishments often provide a safe and social environment, allowing you to meet fellow travelers and gain valuable insights.

b) Consider staying in a pension or guesthouse run by locals. Not only will this provide you with a more authentic experience, but it also offers an opportunity to interact with locals who can offer valuable tips and recommendations.

2. Exploring the Cities:

a) Familiarize yourself with the public transportation system in each city you visit. Turkey has an extensive network of buses, trams, and metros that are not only convenient but also affordable.

b) Join walking tours or hire local guides to explore the cities. This not only ensures you get a deeper understanding of the history and culture but also provides an added layer of safety and companionship.

3. Discovering Historical Sites:

a) Turkey is home to numerous historical sites, such as the ancient city of Ephesus, the stunning landscapes of Cappadocia, and the iconic

Hagia Sophia in Istanbul. Ensure you plan your visits during non-peak hours to avoid crowds and enjoy a more immersive experience.

b) Consider hiring a licensed tour guide to accompany you during your visits to historical sites. They can provide valuable insights, enriching your understanding of Turkey's rich history.

4. Embracing the Local Culture:

a) Engage with locals and immerse yourself in the local culture by visiting local markets, attending cultural events, or dining at local restaurants. Turkey is renowned for its warm hospitality, and solo travelers often find themselves welcomed with open arms.

b) Learn a few basic Turkish phrases. Even a simple merhaba (hello) or te?ekkür ederim (thank you) can go a long way in establishing a connection with locals and making your journey more enjoyable.

5. Staying Safe:

a) While Turkey is generally safe for solo travelers, it is advised to take precautions. Avoid walking alone in poorly lit areas at night and be cautious of your surroundings.

b) Keep your valuables secure and be mindful of pickpockets in crowded areas, especially in popular tourist destinations.

c) Register with your embassy or consulate and keep a copy of your passport and important documents in a safe place.

d) Stay informed about local customs and dress modestly, particularly when visiting religious sites.

Conclusion:

Traveling solo in Turkey can be an incredible adventure, filled with unforgettable experiences. By following these tips and staying vigilant, you can ensure a safe and rewarding journey. Embrace the warmth of Turkish hospitality, immerse yourself in the local culture, and explore the country's rich history. Turkey awaits you with open arms, ready to provide you with a unique and fulfilling solo travel experience

Chapter 42: Tips for Traveling on a Budget in Turkey

Introduction:

Traveling on a budget in Turkey doesn't mean compromising on the quality of your experience. With its rich history, vibrant culture, and stunning landscapes, Turkey offers plenty of opportunities for budget travelers to explore and enjoy. In this chapter, we will provide you with valuable tips on where to stay, things to do, and how to save money while immersing yourself in the beauty of Turkey.

1. Affordable Accommodation Options:

a. Hostels: Turkey is home to numerous budget-friendly hostels that offer comfortable accommodation at affordable prices. These hostels often provide communal spaces, kitchens, and organized activities, making them ideal for meeting fellow travelers.

b. Guesthouses: Opting for guesthouses in smaller towns and rural areas can be a cost-effective choice. These family-run establishments offer a more intimate experience and often include home-cooked meals in their rates.

c. Camping: Turkey boasts picturesque camping spots, especially along its coastal regions. Camping not only saves you money but also allows you to fully immerse yourself in nature's beauty.

2. Exploring on a Budget:

a. Free Attractions: Turkey is dotted with numerous attractions that won't cost you a dime. From exploring the ancient ruins of Ephesus to strolling through the bustling streets of Istanbul's Grand Bazaar, there are plenty of free attractions to keep you entertained.

b. City Passes: Many cities in Turkey offer city passes that provide discounted access to multiple attractions, public transportation, and even dining options. These passes can help you save money while exploring various sites.

c. Local Markets: Instead of dining in expensive restaurants, head to local markets where you can sample delicious street food at a fraction of the price. This way, you can experience authentic Turkish cuisine while staying within your budget.

3. Transportation:

a. Public Transportation: Turkey has an extensive and affordable public transportation system, including buses, trams, and metros. Utilizing these options will save you money compared to hiring private taxis or renting a car.

b. Domestic Flights: If you plan to travel long distances within Turkey, consider booking domestic flights in advance. Many airlines offer discounted fares for early bookings, allowing you to save both time and money.

c. Walking and Cycling: Exploring cities and towns on foot or by bicycle not only saves money but also allows you to discover hidden gems that may be missed when using other forms of transportation.

4. Money-Saving Tips:

a. Bargaining: Bargaining is a common practice in Turkey, especially in markets and bazaars. Don't be afraid to negotiate prices, as it is often expected and can lead to significant savings.

b. Water and Snacks: Carry a reusable water bottle and stock up on snacks from local markets. This will help you avoid unnecessary expenses on bottled water and overpriced snacks at tourist spots.

c. Time your Visit: Traveling during the shoulder seasons (spring and autumn) can result in lower accommodation and flight prices. Additionally, visiting popular attractions early in the morning or later in the day can help you avoid crowds and potentially save on entrance fees.

Conclusion:

Traveling on a budget in Turkey is not only possible but also rewarding. By following these tips, you can explore the diverse landscapes, immerse yourself in the rich culture, and create unforgettable memories without breaking the bank. Remember to plan ahead, embrace local experiences, and make the most of the affordable options available to you. Turkey awaits you with open arms and countless budget-friendly adventures

Chapter 43: Tips for Traveling Responsibly in Turkey

Introduction:

Traveling responsibly is crucial to ensure that we minimize our impact on the environment and culture of the places we visit. In Turkey, a country rich in history, culture, and natural beauty, it becomes even more important to travel responsibly. This chapter aims to provide you with valuable tips and guidelines to help you enjoy your trip to Turkey while being mindful of the environment and culture.

1. Respect the Local Culture:

Turkey has a diverse cultural heritage, and it is essential to respect and appreciate the local customs, traditions, and beliefs. Dress modestly when visiting religious sites like mosques and temples, and be mindful of local customs and etiquette. Engage with locals, learn about their culture, and always be respectful in your interactions.

2. Support Local Businesses:

To minimize your impact on the local economy, prioritize supporting local businesses. Choose locally-owned accommodations, eat at local restaurants that serve traditional cuisine, and shop from local artisans and markets. By doing so, you contribute to the local community's development and preservation of their cultural heritage.

3. Reduce Plastic Waste:

Turkey, like many other countries, faces challenges related to plastic waste. To travel responsibly, carry a reusable water bottle and refill it at water fountains or ask for water refills at restaurants. Avoid single-use plastic items and opt for eco-friendly alternatives. Dispose of your waste properly by using designated recycling bins whenever available.

4. Conserve Water and Energy:

Turkey is prone to water scarcity, especially in certain regions. Be mindful of your water usage, take shorter showers, and turn off the tap while brushing your teeth. Additionally, conserve energy by turning off lights, air conditioning, and other electrical appliances when not in use. These small steps can significantly contribute to the conservation of resources.

5. Choose Sustainable Transportation:

When exploring Turkey, choose sustainable transportation options whenever possible. Utilize public transportation systems like buses, trams, and metros, which are not only eco-friendly but also allow you to experience local life. If you prefer to rent a car, opt for fuel-efficient models and share rides with fellow travelers to reduce carbon emissions.

6. Be Mindful of Wildlife and Nature:

Turkey is blessed with breathtaking landscapes and diverse wildlife. When exploring national parks, nature reserves, or any natural areas, follow designated trails and respect the flora and fauna. Avoid littering, do not disturb wildlife, and refrain from buying products made from endangered species. Admire and appreciate nature's beauty while leaving no trace behind.

7. Learn a Few Local Phrases:

Learning a few basic Turkish phrases can go a long way in building connections with locals and showing respect for their culture. Simple greetings like Merhaba (Hello) and Te?ekkür ederim (Thank you) can help break the ice and create a positive impression. Locals will appreciate your efforts to communicate in their language.

Conclusion:

By following these tips for traveling responsibly in Turkey, you can ensure that your visit leaves a positive impact on the environment and local communities. Remember to respect the local culture, support local businesses, and minimize your ecological footprint. Traveling responsibly not only enriches your own experience but also contributes to the preservation of Turkey's cultural heritage and natural wonders for future generations

www.ingramcontent.com/pod-product-compliance
Lightning Source LLC
Chambersburg PA
CBHW031336160726
47993CB00002B/707